LEARN EXCEL
WITH THE QUALITY
SCORECARD

Ronald N. Goulden, MBA, PMP

Learn Excel with the Quality Scorecard
Copyright © 2011
Ronald N. Goulden, MBA, PMP

ALL RIGHTS RESERVED

Cover design by Ronald Goulden

Microsoft® Excel is a registered trademark of the Microsoft Corporation.

ISBN: 1450557155

Table of Contents

Introduction

There are a lot of books teaching Microsoft® Excel. This is yet another such book… though one with a bit of a twist. The process used by this book will start with a blank worksheet and develop it into a sophisticated Project Management tool called the 'Quality Score Card'.

Do not be alarmed if you are not a Project Manager, the Score Card can be used in other areas, limited only by your imagination. At the very least, this exercise will illustrate the capabilities of Excel and teach some valuable techniques in the process.

The examples in this book are based on Excel 2003 and tested with Excel 2007.

Excel 2007 notes will be italicized and in Franklin Gothic font.

There is no attempt to address the truly unique capabilities of each version of Excel. The goal is to provide fundamental Excel tips and techniques.

Since the functions used in these exercises are pretty standard, they should apply to any spreadsheet application, with slight variations in form and location.

Each chapter builds on previous work so that by the end of the book, you will have a fully functional (and modifiable) Quality Score Card. However, the concepts you learn here will be valuable in any context.

The final chapter discusses the concept of 'Quality by Design', which is the foundation of the Quality Score Card.

This is the first of a series of what I call '**Build-a-Tool**' modules that allow the user to learn Excel techniques while developing fully functional Project Management tools (which may be applicable for other disciplines.)

These modules may ultimately be combined into a single integrated spreadsheet that adheres to the concept of 'enter once, use many' to avoid repetitive and error-prone data entry.

Conventions used in this book

Shaded text represents keys on the keyboard:	
ENTER	Press the ENTER Key.
CTRL	Press and **hold** the CTRL key
ALT	Press and **hold** the ALT key.
SHIFT	Press and **hold** the SHIFT key
TAB	Press the TAB key.
ESC	Press the ESC **key**
DEL	Press the **DEL/ DELETE** key
(Hold the CTRL key while pressing a second key)	
CTRL-C	Copy Selected Text
CTRL-V	Copy Selected Text
CTRL-X	Cut Selected Text
CTRL-D	Copy contents from cell above
Mouse Operations	
{LEFT-CLICK}	Click the **Left** mouse button.
{RIGHT-CLICK}	Click the **Right** mouse button
{DOUBLE-CLICK}	Click the **Left** mouse button **twice** quickly.
Text Options	
Bold words underlined	Menu options, cell references, dialogue boxes, or buttons
'**Bold**' words within quotes	Text to be entered.

Chapter 1

Getting Started

The first step we need to do is start Excel. Excel can be started:

1. From the Microsoft Office Toolbar.
2. From a shortcut on your desktop.
3. By selecting the **Start** button located at the bottom left hand side of your screen and selecting **Programs** then **Microsoft Excel.**

When you start Excel, it should open a blank workbook with two or three blank spreadsheets. If it does not,

[To display the __File__ menus in Excel 2007, {__LEFT-CLICK__} the Windows __logo__ in the upper left corner.]

1. **{LEFT-CLICK}** the **File** menu option.
2. **{LEFT-CLICK} NEW.**
3. **{LEFT-CLICK} Blank Workbook**.
4. **NOTE:** In some versions of Excel, it may be necessary to **{DOUBLE-CLICK} Blank Workbook**.

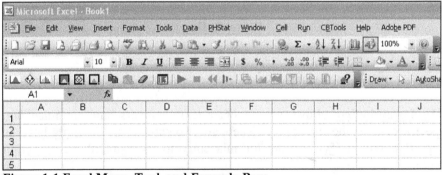

Figure 1-1 Excel <u>Menu</u>, <u>Tool</u>, and <u>Formula Bars</u>

At first glance, an Excel worksheet can be intimidating. However, keep in mind that much of the functionality displayed on the **Menu bar** and the **Tool bars** will not be used.

Depending upon your version of Excel, Figure 1-1 may look different. Do not be concerned, the functionality will be the same.

1

Menu Bar

With that in mind, we can divide the tools (the **Menu bar** and the **Tool bars**) into their relevant components for discussion. The **Menu bar** provides common functions normally seen with other Office applications (**File**, **Edit**, **View**, **Insert**, etc).

Figure 1-2 Menu Bar

Bear in mind that the **Menu bar** for your version of Excel may not match exactly what is displayed in this example, depending upon version, configurations and add-ins.

Tool Bars

Figure 1-3 Tool Bars

Again, what you see on your version of Excel may be different from this example, depending upon your version of Excel and what **Tools** you have enabled.

Formula Bar

Figure 1-4 Formula Bar

The **Formula bar** allows you to enter text, numbers, and formulae into specific cells on the spreadsheet. There are two parts of the **Formula bar**, the **Function** button (**fx**) and the formula entry to the right of the **Function** button

Many buttons in Excel look like pictures, or icons. These are clickable and work exactly like any other on-screen button.

The working area of an Excel Worksheet is made up of cells.

Cells

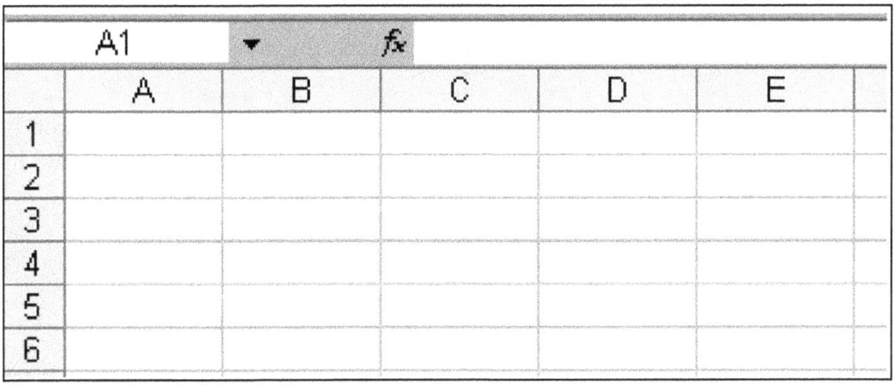

Figure 1-5 Excel Cells (A1)

The cells of a spreadsheet are where the work is performed. While the design may appear confusing, it is really quite simple to navigate a spreadsheet.

Rows are indicated by numbers along the left side of the spreadsheet. **Columns** are represented by letters along the top of the spreadsheet. With this system, any single cell can be referenced as a simple Column/Row designation (Letter/Number). The default cell is always cell **A1**, which is the top row/leftmost column,

In Figure 1-6, cell **C4** is being referenced.

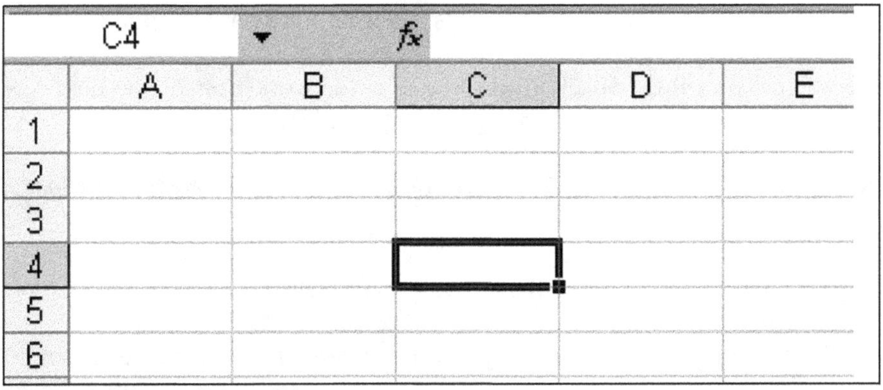

Figure 1-6 Excel Cells - C4

Note that there are three pieces of information to indicate your location in the spreadsheet.
- First, the cell itself is surrounded by a dark, outlining box.
- Second, the left portion of the **Formula bar** says **C4**. (In the previous Figure, it was **A1**.)

3

- Third, row number **4** along the left is shaded, as is column **C** across the top.

Tabs

What most people call a spreadsheet is actually an Excel workbook, which is nothing more than a series of spreadsheet pages (or worksheets) combined in a single document, or file.

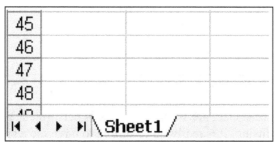

Figure 1-7 Excel tabs

The pages of an Excel workbook contains numerous worksheets, each on its distinct tab. (For the remainder of this discussion, we will refer to the Excel workbook as the spreadsheet, since we will identify the specific pages by their tab identifier.)

The default naming convention for the tabs is: **SHEET1**, **SHEET2**, **SHEET3**, etc). Some versions of Excel will open with three blank tabs while others may open with a single tab. This is a user-configurable option.

The exercises in this book will use two tabs (or worksheets). The next few paragraphs will illustrate how to **Add**, **Delete**, and **Rename** tabs.

[To insert a worksheet in Excel 2007, {LEFT-CLICK} the unnamed tab at the bottom of the screen.]

To **Add** a worksheet or tab to the Excel spreadsheet;

1. {**LEFT-CLICK**} on the **Insert** menu item at the top of the screen.

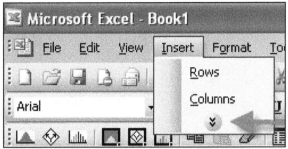
Figure 1-8 <u>Insert</u> Menu Expand button

2. Depending upon your version of Excel, you may have to expand the menu by clicking the double **down-arrow** button as indicated in Figure 1-8.

3. The expanded **<u>Insert</u>** menu will become available as in Figure 1-9.

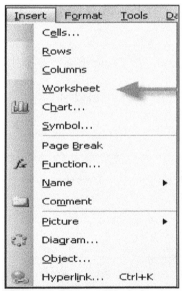
Figure 1-9 <u>Insert</u> Worksheet

4. {**<u>LEFT-CLICK</u>**} on the **<u>Worksheet</u>** menu option and you will see a second tab titled **<u>Sheet2</u>** added to the bottom of the screen.

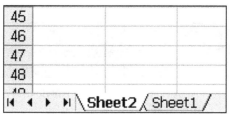
Figure 1-10 Second Worksheet tab added

5. Repeat the process to insert a third worksheet (Figure 1-11).

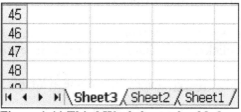
Figure 1-11 Third Worksheet tab added

Now that we have three tabs or worksheet pages available, we need to make the tab names more meaningful. To do this:

1. **{LEFT-CLICK}** on the tab titled **Sheet1**.
2. **{RIGHT-CLICK}** on the tab titled **Sheet1**.
3. A menu similar to Figure 1-12 will appear.

Figure 1-12 Rename menu

4. **{LEFT-CLICK}** the **Rename** option, the tab name (**Sheet1**) will be highlighted (Figure 1-13).

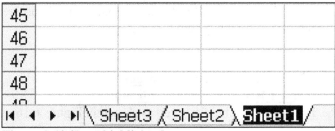
Figure 1-13 Sheet highlighted

5. Type the word **'Cover'** (do not type the single quotes) and press the **ENTER** key.
6. After pressing the **ENTER** key, the tab name has been changed to **Cover**. (Figure 1-14.)

Figure 1-14 Tab renamed to Cover

7. Repeat the process with **Sheet2**, except this time type the word **'Quality'** (do not type the single quotes) and press the **ENTER** key.

Your tabs should look like Figure 1-15. (Do not worry if your tab order is different from what is displayed in Figure 1-15.)

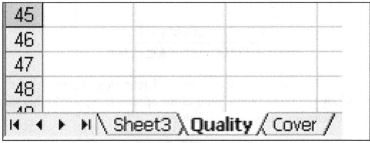
Figure 1-15 Tab renamed to Quality

7

As previously mentioned, we will only use two tabs for this project. So now we need to delete the extra tab, **Sheet3**.

To do this,
1. **{LEFT-CLICK}** the tab titled **Sheet3**.
2. **{RIGHT-CLICK}** the tab titled **Sheet3**.
3. The **Tab** menu will be displayed as shown in Figure 1-16.

Figure 1-16 Tab menu

4. **{LEFT-CLICK}** the **Delete** option and the tab titled **Sheet3** will be removed from the spreadsheet.

   Your tabs should now look similar to Figure 1-17.

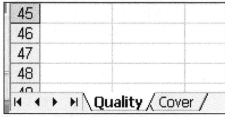

Figure 1-17 Quality and Cover tabs

For one final bit of clean-up work, we will rearrange the order of the tabs. This has no effect on the functioning of the spreadsheet; we do this merely to show how to rearrange tabs in a spreadsheet.

5. **{LEFT-CLICK}** on the tab titled **Cover**.
6. **Hold** the left mouse button down while moving the mouse to the **left**.

7.   Once the cursor is to the **left** of the tab titled **Quality**, release the mouse button.

The tab arrangement should look like Figure 1-18.

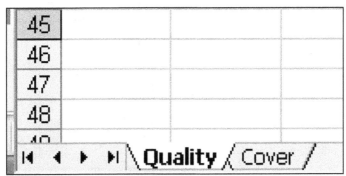
Figure 1-18 <u>Cover</u> & <u>Quality</u> tabs

We will cover a few very important concepts at this time. Saving your work and locating it after you have saved it.

Next, we want to save our work. To do this;
1.   **{LEFT-CLICK}** the **File** menu option.
2.   **{LEFT-CLICK}** the **Save As...** menu option (Figure 1-19).

*[To display the **File** menus in Excel 2007, **{LEFT-CLICK}** the Windows **logo** in the upper left corner.]*

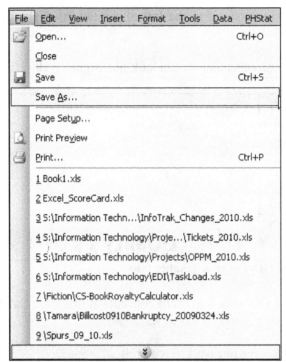

Figure 1-19 File menu

The **Save As** dialogue box will be displayed. (Figure 1-20)

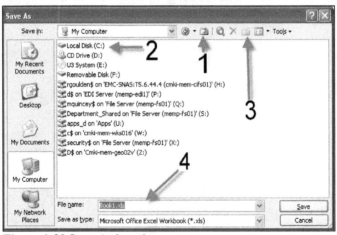

Figure 1-20 Save As location

Looking at Figure 1-20, there are four key points on this dialogue box that we will be concerned with:

1. The **Back Folder** button (**1**) moves backward through the directory structure with each **{LEFT-CLICK}**.
    a. **{LEFT-CLICK}** this button until the **Save In:** box indicates the **Local Disk (C:)**.
2. If the **Save In** box says **My Computer** (or something similar), **{DOUBLE-CLICK}** the left mouse button on **Local Disk (C:)**. The **Save In** box should say, **Local Disk (C:)**.
3. The **Create Folder** button (**3**) allows us to create a new folder.

[In Excel 2007, {LEFT-CLICK} New Folder button.]

4. Since we have not saved the spreadsheet yet, the **File Name** box (**4**) should say **Book1.xls**. (Or something similar, depending on your version of Excel.)

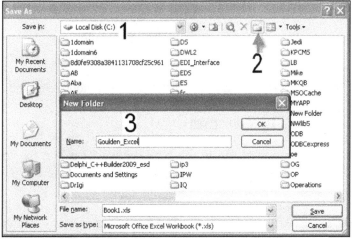

Figure 1-21 Create New Folder

1. Make sure that the **Save In** box (**1**) is referring to **Local Disk (C)**.
2. We want to create a new folder for our work, so **{LEFT-CLICK}** the **Create Folder** button (**2**).
3. The **New Folder** dialogue box (**3**) will display.
4. The **New Folder** box should look similar to Figure 1-21; we will want to change that.
    a. In the **Name** box, type 'Goulden_Excel' (without the single quote marks);
    b. **{LEFT-CLICK}** the **OK** button.
5. Change the **File Name** to 'QUALITY'.

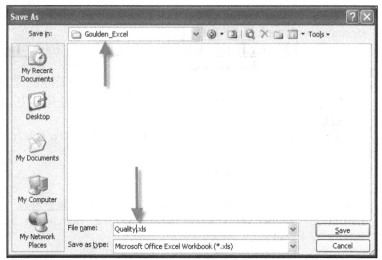

Figure 1-22 <u>Save</u> dialogue

6. In Figure 1-22, the **<u>Save</u>** dialogue box should have changed so that the **<u>Save In</u>** box says **Goulden Excel**, and the **File Name** box should say **Quality.xls**.
7. If not, **{DOUBLE-CLICK}** the **left** mouse button on the **<u>Goulden Excel</u>** directory.
8. **{LEFT-CLICK}** the **<u>Save</u>** button.

Note that the spreadsheet title in the blue (or black) bar at the top of the screen is now **QUALITY.XLS**. [Or just **'Quality'**, depending upon the version of Excel.]

> *[Note for Excel 2007, if you expect to share this with users having older versions of Excel,*
>
> A. *{LEFT-CLICK} the down-arrow for <u>Save as type</u>*
> B. *{LEFT-CLICK} <u>Excel 97-2003 Workbook</u>*
> C. *{LEFT-CLICK} the <u>SAVE</u> button.]*

This will avoid complications for anyone using an older version that needs to access this spreadsheet.

The next thing we want to do is provide information at the bottom of the printed spreadsheet to help us identify the spreadsheet and its location from a printed view. To do this, we must set the footer.

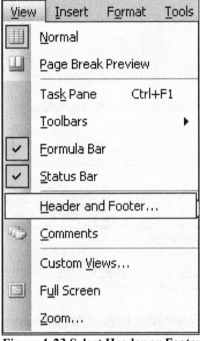

Figure 1-23 Select <u>Header or Footer</u>

1. **{LEFT-CLICK}** the **<u>View</u>** menu option at the top of the screen to display the drop-down menu (Figure 1-23).
2. **{LEFT-CLICK}** on **<u>Header and Footer...</u>**

[In Excel 2007, this is on the **<u>Insert</u>** Tab;
{LEFT-CLICK} <u>Header & Footer</u>.]

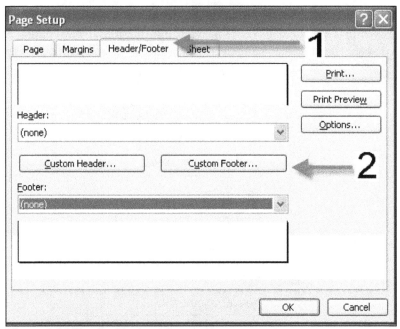

Figure 1-24 Header/Footer tab

3. **{LEFT-CLICK}** the **Custom Footer...** button to display the footer definition dialogue box.

*[In Excel 2007, {LEFT-CLICK} **Go to Footer.**]*

Looking at Figure 1-25, there are six steps required to set our footer.

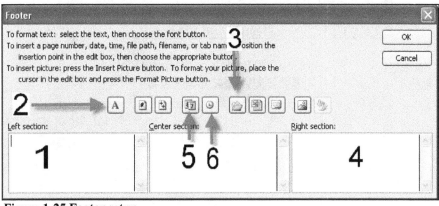

Figure 1-25 Footer setup

1. **{LEFT-CLICK}** the **Left Section (1)**.
2. Referring to Figure 1-25, **{LEFT-CLICK}** the **Path** button **(3)**.

14

3. **{LEFT-CLICK}** the **Right Section (4)**.
4. **{LEFT-CLICK}** the **Current Date** button (**5**), press the **SPACE** key.
5. **{LEFT-CLICK}** The **Current Time** button (**6**).
6. **{DOUBLE-CLICK}** **&[PATH]&[FILE]** in the **Left Section** (it should be highlighted).
7. **{LEFT-CLICK}** the **Font** selection button (**2**).

*[In Excel 2007, this is on the **Home** Tab.]*

To adjust the footer font, looking at Figure 1-27;

1. **{LEFT-CLICK}** the **Font** selection button (**1**).
2. Under the **Font** selection, **{LEFT-CLICK}** the **down-arrow** until you locate the **Arial** font.
3. **{LEFT-CLICK} Arial**.
4. Under **Font Style**, (**2**) **{LEFT-CLICK} Regular**.

[In Excel 2007, this is not available.]

5. Under **Size** (**3**), **{LEFT-CLICK}** the **down-arrow** until you locate the **8** point size.
6. **{LEFT-CLICK}** the '**8**'.
7. Repeat the process with the **&[Date]&[Time]** in the **Right Section**.
8. **{LEFT-CLICK}** the **OK** button.

[In EXCEL 2007, you may need to:
A. {LEFT-CLICK} the **VIEW** tab.
B. **{LEFT-CLICK} NORMAL**.
C. **{LEFT-CLICK} HEADER & FOOTER**.
D. **{LEFT-CLICK} GO TO FOOTER.]*

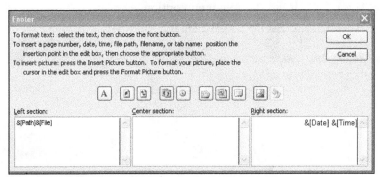

Figure 1-26 Footers selected

The footer selection screen should look similar to Figure 1-26. In the **Left Section**, the **&[Path]&[File]** will now display the path and file name for the spreadsheet, making it easier to locate after printing. (You may not see this change until after saving and reopening the spreadsheet.)

In the **Right Section**, The **&[Date]** displays the date the file was created or changed. By pressing the **SPACE** key, we inserted a blank space between the date and the time (represented by the **&[Time]** in the **Right Section**).

8. **{LEFT-CLICK}** the **OK** button.
9. **{LEFT-CLICK}** the **OK** button again.

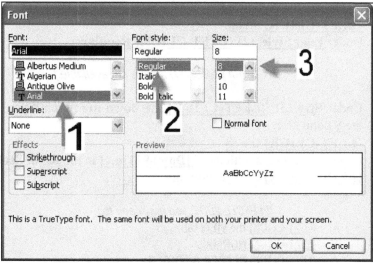

Figure 1-27 Footer <u>Font</u> selection

To confirm that your footer is properly set up,
1. **{LEFT-CLICK}** the **File** menu option.
2. **{LEFT-CLICK}** the **Print Preview** option. (Figure 1-28)

[In Excel 2007, it may be necessary to enter something in a cell on the spreadsheet, just to have something to print.]

16

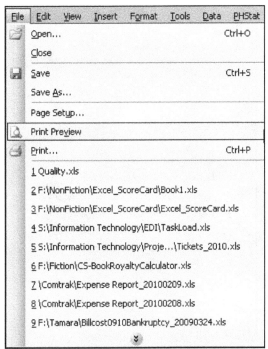

Figure 1-28 **Print Preview** menu selection

The footer should look similar to Figure 1-29.

C:\Goulden_Excel\Quality.xls   2/8/2010 1:05 PM

Figure 1-29 Footer information

3. **{LEFT-CLICK}** the **Close Preview** button at the top of the screen.

It is a wise practice to **always** include this information at the bare minimum. When you have hundreds of spreadsheets located in dozens of directories, it can complicate the task of locating a specific spreadsheet upon demand. However, with a footer that identifies the file name and path, it becomes a simple task to locate the spreadsheet on a moment's notice.

With the basics of Excel out of the way, we can move forward with the learning process. By the end of this book, your spreadsheet will look almost exactly like the one on the cover of the book.

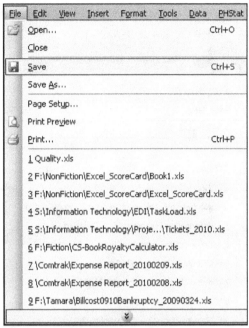

Figure 1-30 Save menu option.

To save to your work:

    1. **{LEFT-CLICK}** the **File** menu item at the top of the screen.
    2. **{LEFT-CLICK}** the **Save** option.

Since we have already defined the file name and file path for our file, we can now save our work with a simple **{LEFT-CLICK}** of the **File** menu item and a **{LEFT-CLICK}** on the **Save** menu option. (Figure 1-30).

[For Excel 2007, {LEFT-CLICK} the logo in the upper left corner.]

Close the spreadsheet.

    1. **{LEFT-CLICK}** the **File** menu item at the top of the screen.
    2. **{LEFT-CLICK}** the **Close** option.

The spreadsheet should not be visible.

Close Excel by:

    1. **{LEFT-CLICK}** the **X** at the **upper** right corner of the screen.
    2. Or **{LEFT-CLICK}** the **File** menu item at the top of the screen.
    3. **{LEFT-CLICK}** the **Exit Excel** option.

Chapter 2

Titles and Headers

In this chapter, we will work with basic titles and headers. We will not worry about formatting yet, we will merely try to put the basic information on the spreadsheet.

Re-open the spreadsheet.

1. **{LEFT-CLICK}** the **File** menu item at the top of the screen.
2. **{LEFT-CLICK}** the **Open** option.
3. **{LEFT-CLICK}** the **Quality** spreadsheet file.
4. **{LEFT-CLICK}** the **Open** button.

Note: depending on your version of Excel, you may need to 'navigate' to the **C:\Goulden_Excel** directory.

For most of the exercises in this book, we will be using the **Quality** tab. With that in mind,

1. **{LEFT-CLICK}** on the tab titled **Quality**.
2. **{LEFT-CLICK}** cell **A3** .
3. Type '**QS**', then press the TAB key.
4. Cell **B3** should be highlighted.
5. Type '**Quality Scorecard**'. (Figure 2-1.)

B3	▼	*fx*	Quality Scorecard	
	A	B	C	D
1				
2				
3	QS	Quality Scorecard		
4				

Figure 2-1 Cell B3

In looking at Figure 2-1, there are some interesting aspects to consider.

- First, the upper left corner of the Figure has **B3** in the white box. This value will change as you move around the spread sheet. Press the TAB key and notice that the value changes to **C3**. Hold the SHIFT key down while pressing the TAB key and the value will change back to **B3**.

- Second, note that the actual cell **B3** has a black box around it. This indicates that it is the active cell being edited. The active cell is the one with the cursor (or black box surrounding it.)

- Third, the words 'Quality Scorecard' crosses over into cell **C3**. (Do not worry about this, it is not a problem.)

- Fourth, the **Formula bar** (the white area at the top of the screen and to the left of the **fx** button has the words '**Quality Scorecard**' in it. The **Formula bar** will always display the text or formula for each active cell.

1. {LEFT-CLICK} on the **fx** button to display a drop-down list of functions.
2. {LEFT-CLICK} the **Cancel** button.

Next, we will create the header and sub-header for the spreadsheet.

1. {LEFT-CLICK} cell **B4**.
2. While Holding the **CTRL** key down, press the **D** key.

Note that the contents of the cell immediately above (**B3**) have been duplicated into cell **B4**. The **CRTL-D** key combination duplicates the contents of the cell above into the active cell.

3. {LEFT-CLICK} cell **B5**.
4. {LEFT-CLICK} in the white **Formula bar** at the top of the screen.
5. Type '**GSC-17 Module Data Collection and Reporting**' in the **Formula bar** and press the **ENTER** key. (Figure 2-2.) (Do not type the single quote characters.)

fx | GSC-17 Module Data Collection and Reporting

Figure 2-2 **Formula Bar** entry

With the basic headers set up, we can do a little preliminary house-keeping. The first thing we will do is adjust the size of column **A**. There are a number of ways to do this, but the easiest is to:

1. Move the cursor to the line separating column **A** from column **B**.
2. {LEFT-CLICK} and **hold** the left mouse button down while moving the mouse to the **left**, reducing the width of column **A** until the contents of cell **A3** just fit within the cell borders.
3. Release the **left** mouse button.

20

We will perform a similar operation on column **B**:

1. Move the cursor to the line separating column **B** from column **C**.
2. {**LEFT-CLICK**} and **hold** the **left** mouse button down while moving the mouse to the **right**.
3. When the contents of cell **B3** barely fits within the borders, release the **left** mouse button.

	A	B	C	D	E
1					
2					
3	QS	Quality Scorecard			
4		Quality Scorecard			
5		GSC-17 Module Data Collection and Reporting			

Figure 2-3 Resized cells

Note in Figure 2-3 that column **A** is much smaller and column **B** is much larger than the other columns. We have just adjusted the column sizes to match the data.

Our next operation will be to center the header and sub-header on our spreadsheet. To do this:

1. {**LEFT-CLICK**} cell **B4.**
2. **Hold** the **SHIFT** key down while repeatedly pressing the **right arrow** key (→) until you reach column **AC**. (Make sure that the **Scroll Lock** is not on.)
3. {**LEFT-CLICK**} the **Merge/Center** button on the toolbar (Figure 2-4).

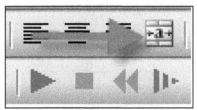

Figure 2-4 Merge/Center button

*[In Excel 2007, this is on the **Home** Tab.]*

1. {**LEFT-CLICK**} cell **B5.**

21

2. Hold the **SHIFT** key down while repeatedly pressing the **right arrow** key (→) until you reach column **AC**. (Make sure that the **Scroll Lock** is not on.)
3. {**LEFT-CLICK**} the **Merge/Center** button on the toolbar (Figure 2-4).

Note that '**Quality Scorecard**' and '**GSC-17 Module Data Collection and Reporting**' both moved to the right and are centered with each other.

If you {**LEFT-CLICK**} on either phrase, the contents are displayed in the **Formula bar**. However, the cell reference to the left of the formula bar reports **B4** and **B5**, respectively.

This process has centered the heading and sub-heading on our spreadsheet.

The next step in our spreadsheet development is to provide the row labels (headers) for rows **10** through **32**.

1. {**LEFT-CLICK**} cell **B10**.
2. Type "**Database Flaws**" then press the **ENTER** key. The cursor should automatically move to cell **B11**. If it does not, we can easily correct that.

Let's assume that the cursor moved to cell **C10** after pressing the **ENTER** key. To control the cursor direction:

1. {**LEFT-CLICK**} on the **Tools** menu item at the top of the screen as shown in Figure 2-5.

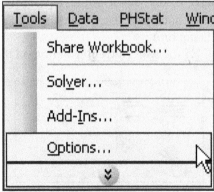

Figure 2-5 Options menu selection

2. When you {**LEFT-CLICK**} **Options**, a display similar to Figure 2-6 will be presented.

22

[For Excel 2007,
- A. *{LEFT-CLICK} the **logo** in the upper left corner.*
- B. *{LEFT-CLICK} the **Excel Options** button.*
- C. *{LEFT-CLICK} the **Advanced** button.*
- D. *Change the **direction** to **Down.***
- E. *{LEFT-CLICK} the **OK** button.*

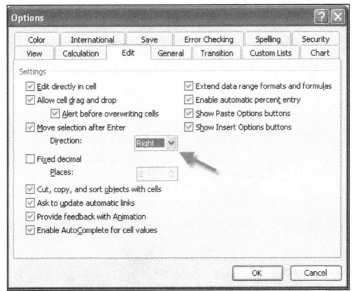

Figure 2-6 <u>Right</u> direction selected

If the cursor moved to the right (cell **<u>C10</u>**) when you pressed the **ENTER** key, then the direction is set to the **<u>Right</u>** as shown in Figure 2-6. To change the exit direction:

1. **{LEFT-CLICK}** the **down-arrow** (beside the word **<u>Right</u>**).
2. Select **<u>Down</u>**. The screen should look similar to Figure 2-7.
3. If the direction is set to **<u>Down</u>,** press the **ENTER** key.

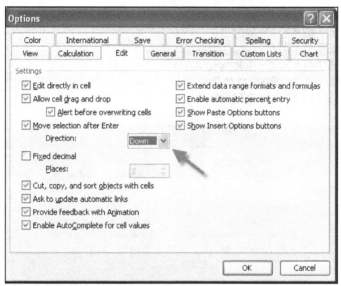

Figure 2-7 <u>Down</u> direction selected

1. **{LEFT-CLICK}** cell **B10**.
2. Press the **ENTER** key.

Now when you press the **ENTER** key, the cursor will move down, simplifying data entry.

To resume entering our row titles,

3. **{LEFT-CLICK}** cell **B11**.
4. Type '**Screen Errors**' and press the **ENTER** key. (The cursor should have automatically moved to cell **B12**).

Do not worry about the meanings of these titles, just type them as listed. The goal is to teach Excel fundamentals while producing a working spreadsheet. Your finished spreadsheet should look similar to the one on the cover of the book.

Type '**Report Errors**'	Press the **ENTER** key
Type '**Scope Shortages**'	Press the **ENTER** key
Type '**Program Logic Errors**'	Press the **ENTER** key
Type '**Redesign**'	Press the **ENTER** key
Type '**Scope Change**'	Press the **ENTER** key
Type '**Missing Objects**'	Press the **ENTER** key
Type '**Level Checks**'	Press the **ENTER** key
Type '**Extraneous Objects**'	Press the **ENTER** key

Type 'Gold Plating'	Press the ENTER key
Type 'Pre-existing Conditions'	Press the ENTER key
Type 'Critical Errors'	Press the ENTER key
Type 'Installation Errors'	Press the ENTER key
Type 'Training Issues'	Press the ENTER key
Type 'Environmental Issues'	Press the ENTER key
Type 'Cosmetic Changes'	Press the ENTER key
Type 'Data Errors'	Press the ENTER key
Type 'Implementation/Setup'	Press the ENTER key
Type 'User Error'	Press the ENTER key
Type 'Application Errors'	Press the ENTER key
Type 'Typographical Errors'	Press the ENTER key
Type 'T/O Omissions'	Press the ENTER key

The cursor should be in cell **B33**. Check your spelling and make any corrections necessary.

	A	B	C
1			
2			
3	QS	Quality Scorecard	
4			
5			
6			
7			
8			
9			
10		Database Flaws	
11		Screen Errors	
12		Report Errors	
13		Scope Shortages	
14		Program Logic Errors	
15		Redesign	
16		Scope Change	
17		Missing Objects	
18		Level Checks	
19		Extraneous Objects	
20		Gold Plating	
21		Pre-existing Conditions	
22		Critical Errors	
23		Installation Errors	
24		Training Issues	
25		Environmental Issues	
26		Cosmetic Changes	
27		Data Errors	
28		Implementation/Setup	
29		User Error	
30		Application Errors	
31		Typographical Errors	
32		T/O Omissions	

2-8 Row Titles

Since the titles are different lengths, some of them may overlap into column **C**. To correct this:

1. Move the cursor to the line separating the **B** and **C** column headers at the top of the screen.
2. {**LEFT-CLICK**} on the line and **hold** the **left** mouse button down while moving the mouse to the **right** until all of the text on the rows fit within the column **B** borders.
3. Release the **left** mouse button.

	A	B	C
1			
2			
3	QS	Quality Scorecard	
4			
5			
6			
7			
8			
9			
10		Database Flaws	
11		Screen Errors	
12		Report Errors	
13		Scope Shortages	
14		Program Logic Errors	
15		Redesign	
16		Scope Change	
17		Missing Objects	
18		Level Checks	
19		Extraneous Objects	
20		Gold Plating	
21		Pre-existing Conditions	
22		Critical Errors	
23		Installation Errors	
24		Training Issues	
25		Environmental Issues	
26		Cosmetic Changes	
27		Data Errors	
28		Implementation/Setup	
29		User Error	
30		Application Errors	
31		Typographical Errors	
32		T/O Omissions	

Figure 2-9 Adjusted Row Titles

We need to add one more row title in cell **B41**.
1. **{LEFT-CLICK}** cell **B41.**
2. Type '**Totals:**' and press the **ENTER** key.

There is one final step we need to perform to complete entry of our headers and titles. We need to add headers for the quality categories.

3. **{LEFT-CLICK}** cell **C9**.

We want to simplify our data entry by making the cursor automatically move to the **right** when we press the **ENTER** key. To do this, we will reverse the process we did earlier.

1. **{LEFT-CLICK}** the **Tools** menu.
2. **{LEFT-CLICK} Options**. (Figure 2-10.)

27

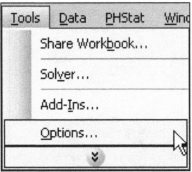

Figure 2-10 Selecting Options

3. **{LEFT-CLICK}** the **Options** selection to display a screen similar to Figure 2-11.

Since we previously set the cursor direction to **Down**, we need to change the direction to **Right**.

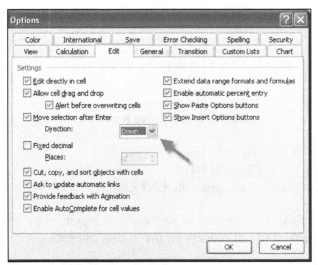

Figure 2-11 Down is selected

4. **{LEFT-CLICK}** the **down-arrow** (beside the word **Down**) and select **Right**.

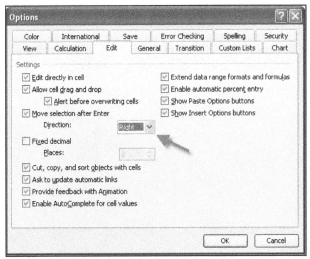

Figure 2-12 Right is selected

5. After ensuring that the cursor direction is set to **Right**, press the **ENTER** key.

[For Excel 2007,
A. {LEFT-CLICK} the logo in the upper left corner.
B. {LEFT-CLICK} the Excel Options button.
C. {LEFT-CLICK} the Advanced button.
D. Change the direction to Right.
E. {LEFT-CLICK} the OK button.]

1. **{LEFT-CLICK}** cell **C9** and type **'DQ'** then press the **ENTER** key. The cursor should have moved to the **right** to cell **D9**.

All of these entries should be uppercase.

Type **'OQ**	Press the **ENTER** key
Type **'PQ**	Press the **ENTER** key
Type **'IQ'**	Press the **ENTER** key
Type **'QA'**	Press the **ENTER** key
Type **'QA'**	Press the **ENTER** key
Type **'QA'**	Press the **ENTER** key
Type **'QA'**	Press the **ENTER** key
Type **'HD'**	Press the **ENTER** key
Type **'HD'**	Press the **ENTER** key
Type **'HD'**	Press the **ENTER** key
Type **'HD'**	Press the **ENTER** key

29

The cursor should be in cell **O9**.

Your spreadsheet should look like Figure 2-13.

	A	B	C	D	E	F	G	H	I	J	K	L	M	N	O
1															
2															
3	QS	Quality Scorecard													
4														Quality Scor	
5													GSC-17 Module Data Colle		
6															
7															
8			DQ	OQ	PQ	IQ	QA	QA	QA	QA	HD	HD	HD	HD	
9															
10		Database Flaws													
11		Screen Errors													
12		Report Errors													
13		Scope Shortages													
14		Program Logic Errors													
15		Redesign													
16		Scope Change													
17		Missing Objects													
18		Level Checks													
19		Extraneous Objects													
20		Gold Plating													
21		Pre-existing Conditions													
22		Critical Errors													
23		Installation Errors													
24		Training Issues													
25		Environmental Issues													
26		Cosmetic Changes													
27		Data Errors													
28		Implementation/Setup													
29		User Error													
30		Application Errors													
31		Typographical Errors													
32		T/O Omissions													

Figure 2-13 Title Entry finished

While it may not look like much, a good portion of the spreadsheet development is finished. In the next chapter, we will work on formatting the spreadsheet and making it more presentable.

We do have a few more headers to add. But we will include those in Chapter Three.

Save your work.

30

Chapter 3

Borders and Formatting

Without borders and formatting, an Excel spreadsheet is pretty unspectacular. In this chapter, we will begin to make the spreadsheet into more of a 'presentation quality' document.

The first thing we will do is define the 'major' border.

1. **{LEFT-CLICK}** cell **AC41.**
2. **Hold** the left mouse button down while moving the cursor **upward** and to the **left**, stopping at cell **B8**.
3. Release the **left** mouse button.

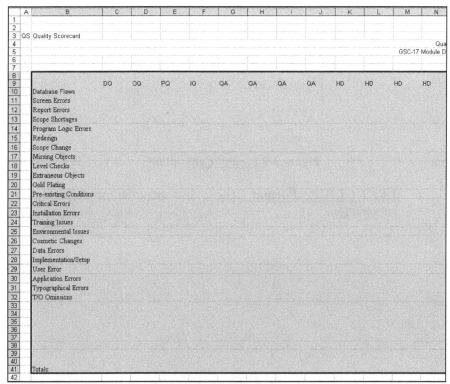

Figure 3-1 Major Border area selected

When the mouse button is released, the area on the spreadsheet from cell **B8** to **AC41** is selected (highlighted) as shown in Figure 3-1.

31

4. **{RIGHT-CLICK}** the (**right**) mouse button to display the **Options** menu.

5. Move the cursor to the **Format Cells...** option (Figure 3-2).

Figure 3-2 Format Cells option

6. **{LEFT-CLICK}** **Format Cells...** to display the formatting options screen (Figure 3-3).

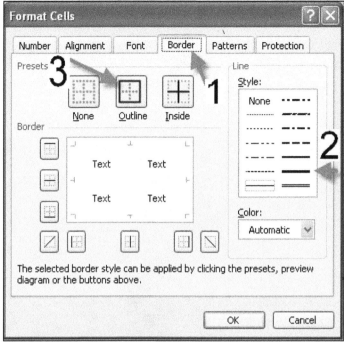

Figure 3-3 Format Cells screen

Looking at this screen, there are several tabs at the top (**Number, Alignment, Font, Border, Patterns, and Protection**). We will use most of these in the course of this chapter's exercises.

However, the one we are most interested in at this time is the **Border** tab.

7. **{LEFT-CLICK}** the **Border** tab. (Arrow number (**1**) in Figure 3-3.)

The next action we want to do is select the line style and weight (thickness). Since this is the primary (or major) border, we want to select the heaviest weight, which is indicated by the number (**2**) in Figure 3-3.

8. **{LEFT-CLICK}** the thickest line (number (**2**)).

Below the line style, we have to option to select the line color. However, at this time, we will use the automatic color selection, which is black. We do not need to do anything with color selection at this time.

The last thing we need to do is apply the line selection to our area. To do this,

9. **{LEFT-CLICK}** the **Outline** symbol as indicated by the number (**3**) in Figure 3-3.

33

10. {LEFT-CLICK} the **OK** button and the spreadsheet area we previously selected now has a heavy outlined border as shown in Figure 3-4.
11. **LEFT-CLICK** a cell outside of the selection area.

	A	B	C	D	E	F	G	H	I	J	K	L	M	N
1														
2														
3	QS	Quality Scorecard												
4														
5													GSC-17 Modul	
6														
7														
8														
9			DQ	OQ	PQ	IQ	QA	QA	QA	QA	HD	HD	HD	HD
10		Database Flaws												
11		Screen Errors												
12		Report Errors												
13		Scope Shortages												
14		Program Logic Errors												
15		Redesign												
16		Scope Change												
17		Missing Objects												
18		Level Checks												
19		Extraneous Objects												
20		Gold Plating												
21		Pre-existing Conditions												
22		Critical Errors												
23		Installation Errors												
24		Training Issues												
25		Environmental Issues												
26		Cosmetic Changes												
27		Data Errors												
28		Implementation/Setup												
29		User Error												
30		Application Errors												
31		Typographical Errors												
32		T/O Omissions												

Figure 3-4 Major Border applied

Note that in Figure 3-4 the entire spreadsheet is not displayed. This is for readability; your area **B8** to **AC41** should have a solid black border around it.

The next step is to place borders around the secondary areas. The first is cells **C9** through **N41**.

1. **{LEFT-CLICK}** on cell **N41**.
2. **Hold** the **left** mouse button down while moving the cursor **upwards** and to the **left**, stopping at cell **C9**.
3. Upon releasing the **left** mouse button, the area from **C9** through **N41** is selected (highlighted) as shown in Figure 3-5.
4. **{RIGHT-CLICK}** the selected area and the **Options** menu will be displayed (Figure 3-2).
5. **{LEFT-CLICK}** the **Format Cells...** option to access the formatting screen. (Make sure you are on the **Border** tab.)

The next action we want to do is select the line style and weight (thickness). Since this is the primary (or major) border, we want to

34

6. Select the heaviest weight line, which is indicated by the number (**2**) in Figure 3-3.

Below the line style, we have to option to select the line color. Again, we will use the automatic color selection, which is black. We do not need to do anything with color selection at this time.

7. The last thing we need to do is apply the line selection to our area. To do this, **{LEFT-CLICK}** the **<u>Outline</u>** symbol as indicated by the number (**3**) in Figure 3-3.
8. **{LEFT-CLICK}** the **<u>OK</u>** button and the spreadsheet area we selected now has a heavy outlined border as shown in Figure 3-5.

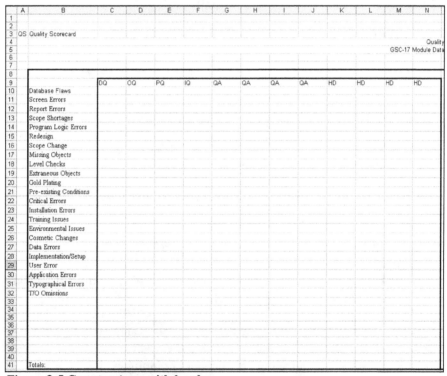

Figure 3-5 Counter Area with border

Still working with the area we just outlined,

9. **{LEFT-CLICK}** cell **<u>C9.</u>**
10. **Hold** the **SHIFT** key down.
11. **{LEFT-CLICK}** cell **<u>N9.</u>**
12. Release the mouse button.

Note that the area from **<u>C9</u>** through **<u>N9</u>** is selected.

13. Move the cursor to the top of the screen.
14. {LEFT-CLICK} the **Bold** tool (the letter **B**) (Figure 3-6.)

Figure 3-6 Bold tool button

*[In Excel 2007, this is on the **Home** Tab.]*

This changes the text of the selected area from **normal** to **bold**.

15. {LEFT-CLICK} the **Center** tool, as shown in Figure 3-7.

Figure 3-7 Center tool button

With those two button clicks, you have made the text **bold** and **centered** it within each cell.

16. With the same area still selected, {RIGHT-CLICK} to bring up the options menu.
17. {LEFT-CLICK} the **Format Cells...** option (Figure 3-2). (Make sure you are on the **Border** tab.)

The next action we want to do is select the line style and weight (thickness). Since this is the primary (or major) border, we want to select the heaviest weight line, which is indicated by the number (**2**) in Figure 3-3.

Below the line style, we have to option to select the line color. We do not need to do anything with color selection at this time.

Now, we need to apply the line selection to our area. To do this:

18. {LEFT-CLICK} the **Outline** symbol as indicated by the number (**3**) in Figure 3-3.

Next, we want to set the inside lines for this selected area. To do this:

19. **{LEFT-CLICK}** the line style above the bold one we have used so far (arrow number (**1**)) in Figure 3-8.
20. **{LEFT-CLICK}** the **Inside** symbol as indicated by number (**2**).

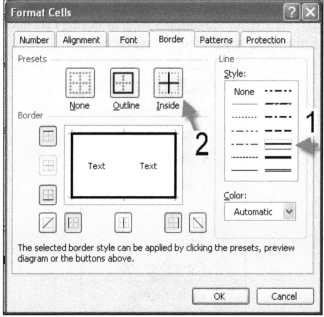

Figure 3-8 Lighter Border selection

1. **{LEFT-CLICK}** the **OK** button.
2. **{LEFT-CLICK}** a cell outside of the selection area.

Note that the spreadsheet area we selected now has a heavy outlined border and slightly lighter inside borders as shown in Figure 3-9.

DQ	OQ	PQ	IQ	QA	QA	QA	QA	HD	HD	HD	HD

Figure 3-9 Inside borders

We still have a little work to do on these headers.

1. Move the cursor to the top of the screen.
2. **{LEFT-CLICK}** on the column header **C**.
3. **Hold** the **SHIFT** key down.
4. **{LEFT-CLICK}** on column header **N**. Columns **C** through **N** will be selected (highlighted) as shown in Figure 3-10.

37

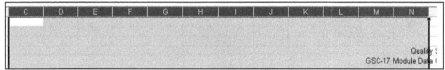

Figure 3-10 Columns C through N selected

5. **{RIGHT-CLICK}** the selected **column headers** (**C** through **N**) and the **Column Options** menu will appear as shown in Figure 3-11.

Figure 3-11 Column Width menu option

6. **{LEFT-CLICK}** the **Column Width...** option to display the **Column Width** setting screen (Figure 3-12).

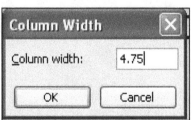

Figure 3-12 Setting Column Width

7. In the **Column Width** box, type '**4.75**'.

38

8. {LEFT-CLICK} the OK button.

The selected columns will 'shrink' as shown in Figure 3-13.

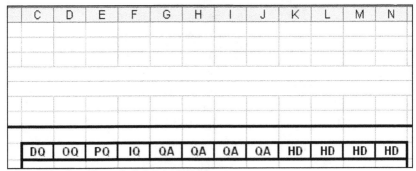

Figure 3-13 Adjusted <u>Column Widths</u>

Next, we will adjust the row headers.

1. **{LEFT-CLICK}** cell **B10**.
2. **Hold** the **SHIFT** key down.
3. **{LEFT-CLICK}** cell **B41**. The selected area will be highlighted.

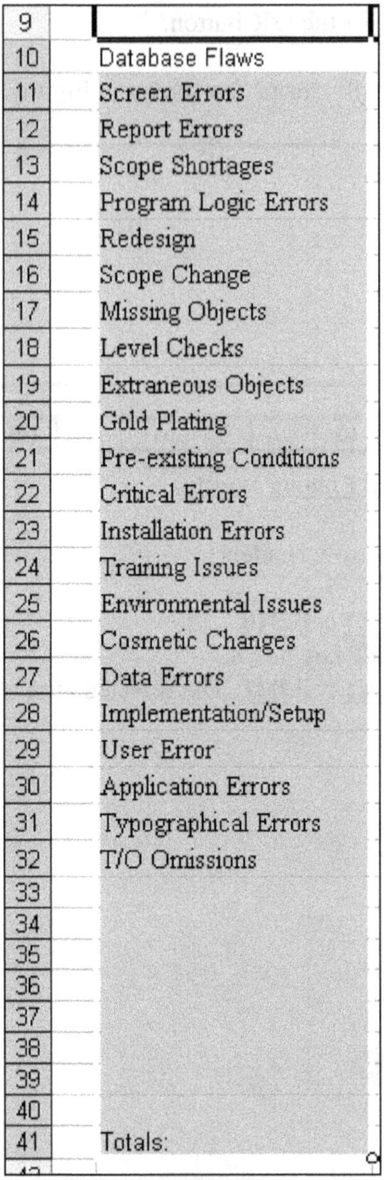

9	
10	Database Flaws
11	Screen Errors
12	Report Errors
13	Scope Shortages
14	Program Logic Errors
15	Redesign
16	Scope Change
17	Missing Objects
18	Level Checks
19	Extraneous Objects
20	Gold Plating
21	Pre-existing Conditions
22	Critical Errors
23	Installation Errors
24	Training Issues
25	Environmental Issues
26	Cosmetic Changes
27	Data Errors
28	Implementation/Setup
29	User Error
30	Application Errors
31	Typographical Errors
32	T/O Omissions
33	
34	
35	
36	
37	
38	
39	
40	
41	Totals:

Figure 3-14 Row Headers selected

4. **{LEFT-CLICK}** the **Bold** tool button (Figure 3-6).
5. **{LEFT-CLICK}** on the **Right-Adjust** tool button (Figure 3-15).

40

Figure 3-15 <u>Right Adjust</u> tool button

At this point, the spreadsheet should look similar to Figure 3-16.

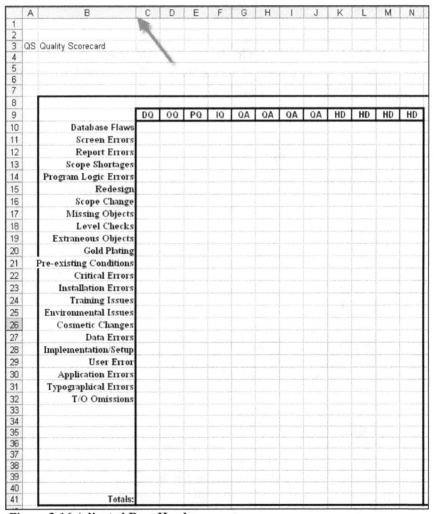

Figure 3-16 Adjusted Row Headers

Note: If some of the row headers overlap the border (as is the case with row **21**, 'Pre-existing Conditions' in Figure 3-16), the problem can be easily corrected; **{DOUBLE-CLICK}** (click the **left** mouse button two times, quickly) on the line separating columns **B** and **C** as indicated by the arrow at the top of Figure 3-16. Doing so will adjust the column to the widest element in the column.

Moving forward, we have a few more borders to set and some font adjustments.

1. **{LEFT-CLICK}** on cell **B41**.
2. **Hold** the **SHIFT** key down.
3. **{LEFT-CLICK}** cell **N41**.
4. **{RIGHT-CLICK}** the selected area to bring up the **Options** menu.
5. **{LEFT-CLICK}** the **Format Cells...** option (Figure 3-2). (Make sure you are on the **Border** tab.)

The next action we want to do is select the line style and weight (thickness). Since this is the primary (or major) border, we want to select the heaviest weight, which is indicated by the number (**2**) in Figure 3-3.

Now, we need to do is apply the line selection to our area. To do this;

1. **{LEFT-CLICK}** the **Outline** symbol as indicated by the number (**3**) in Figure 3-3.

Next, we want to set the inside lines for this selected area. To do this;

2. **{LEFT-CLICK}** the line style above the bold one we have used so far (arrow (**1**)) in Figure 3-8.
3. **{LEFT-CLICK}** the **Inside** symbol as indicated by arrow number (**2**).
4. **{LEFT-CLICK}** the **OK** button and the spreadsheet area we had previously selected has a heavy outlined border and slightly lighter inside borders.
5. **{LEFT-CLICK}** cell **C10**.
6. **Hold** the **SHIFT** key down.
7. **{LEFT-CLICK}** cell **N40**.
8. **{RIGHT-CLICK}** the selected area to bring up the options menu.
9. **{LEFT-CLICK}** the **Format Cells...** option (Figure 3-2).

The next action we want to do is select the line **Style** and **Weight** (thickness).

10. Since this is the interior data range, we want to select the lightest weight, which is indicated by the number (**1**) in Figure 3-17.

Next, we want to set the inside lines for this selected area.

11. Then **{LEFT-CLICK}** the **Inside** symbol as indicated by arrow number (**2**).

12. **{LEFT-CLICK}** the **OK** button.

The selected spreadsheet area now has a heavy outlined border and slightly lighter inside borders.

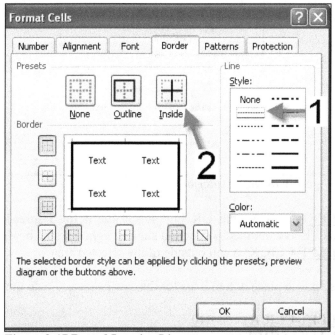

Figure 3-17 Dotted Interior Lines

1. **{LEFT-CLICK}** cell **G10**.
2. **Hold** the **SHIFT** key down.
3. **{LEFT-CLICK}** cell **J40**.
4. **{RIGHT-CLICK}** the selected area to bring up the options menu.
5. **{LEFT-CLICK}** the **Format Cells...** option (Figure 3-2).

Again, we want to select the line **style** and **weight** (thickness). Since this data range separates functional groupings, we want to select a heavier weight line, which is indicated by the number (**1**) in Figure 3-18.

6. {LEFT-CLICK} on the **left** and **right** borders as indicated by the arrows numbered (**2**) in Figure 3-18.

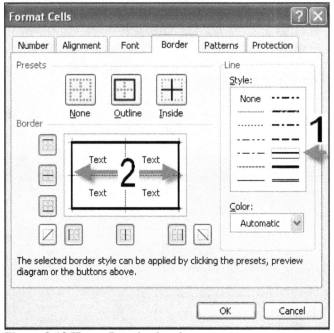

Figure 3-18 Heavy Interior borders

7. {LEFT-CLICK} the **OK** button and the defined spreadsheet area has a heavy outlined border and slightly lighter inside borders.
8. {LEFT-CLICK} a cell outside of the selected area.

The next step is to place dotted lines for the row headers. To do this:

1. {LEFT-CLICK} cell **B10**.
2. **Hold** the **SHIFT** key down.
3. {LEFT-CLICK} cell **B40**.
4. {RIGHT-CLICK} the selected area to bring up the options menu.
5. {LEFT-CLICK} the **Format Cells...** option (Figure 3-2).
6. {LEFT-CLICK} the dotted line style (arrow number (**1**)) in Figure 3-17.
7. {LEFT-CLICK} the **Inside** symbol indicated by arrows number (**2**).
8. {LEFT-CLICK} the **OK** button and the row headers have dotted lines separating them.

Now we will adjust the spreadsheet headers.

1. {LEFT-CLICK} cell **A3**.
2. **Hold** the **SHIFT** key down.
3. {LEFT-CLICK} cell **B3**.
4. {RIGHT-CLICK} the selected area to bring up the options menu.
5. {LEFT-CLICK} the **Format Cells...** option (Figure 3-2).
6. {LEFT-CLICK} the **Border** tab.
7. {LEFT-CLICK} the **Font** tab.
8. Select the **Tahoma** font.
   a. {LEFT-CLICK} the slider bar on the right of the **Font** selection box
   b. **Hold** the **left** mouse button down while dragging the 'slider' **downward** until you see **Tahoma**.
   c. {LEFT-CLICK} the **Tahoma** font.
9. {LEFT-CLICK} **Font style** = **Bold**,
10. {LEFT-CLICK} **Size** = **18**.
11. {LEFT-CLICK} the **down-arrow** in the color selection box and select the **dark gray** color, as indicated by the arrow in Figure 3-19.

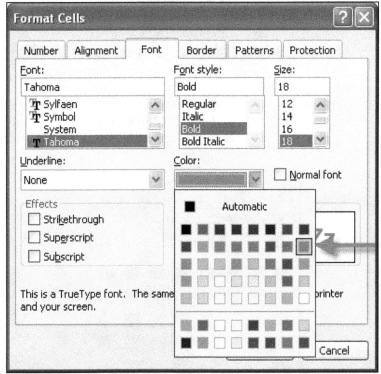

Figure 3-19 Font Change screen

[This will appear differently in Excel 2007.]

45

12. {LEFT-CLICK} the OK button.

NOTE: You may need to adjust the column widths.

With the header and sub-header, we will adjust the font using a different technique.

Figure 3-20 Tool Bar Font change

1. {LEFT-CLICK} cell B4.

Looking at Figure 3-20, adjust the font according to the following arrow steps:

2. Arrow (0) – {LEFT-CLICK} the Arial font style.
   a. {LEFT-CLICK} the down-arrow to the right of the Font selection box to display a list of fonts.
3. Arrow (1) – {LEFT-CLICK} the font Size to 24.
4. Arrow ((2) – {LEFT-CLICK} the Bold tool bar button.
5. Arrow (3) – {LEFT-CLICK} the Center tool bar button.
6. Arrow (4) –This button indicates this is a merged cell, do nothing.
7. Arrow (5) – {LEFT-CLICK} the down-arrow to the right of the text Color tool bar button to display the color selection menu in Figure 3-21.

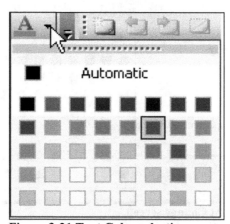

Figure 3-21 Text Color selection

46

On the text color selection screen,

8. {LEFT-CLICK} the next to the darkest **blue** (second from the top, third from the right).
9. {LEFT-CLICK} cell **B5** and repeat the process except on arrow number (**1**), set the font size = **20**.
10. **LEFT-CLICK}** cell **A3.**
11. Hold the SHIFT key down.
12. **LEFT-CLICK}** cell **B3**.
13. {RIGHT-CLICK} the selected area to bring up the options menu.
14. {LEFT-CLICK} the **Format Cells...** option (Figure 3-2).
15. {LEFT-CLICK} the **Border** tab.

Looking at Figure 3-22,

1. {LEFT-CLICK} the heaviest line style as indicated by arrow number (**1**).
2. {LEFT-CLICK} the **down-arrow** by the color selection.
3. {LEFT-CLICK} the next to the lightest **gray** as indicated by arrow number (**3**).
4. {LEFT-CLICK} the **bottom border** as indicated by arrow number (**2**).
5. {LEFT-CLICK} the **OK** button.

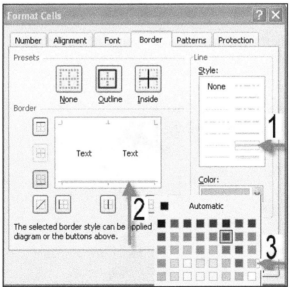

Figure 3-22 Line Color selection

At this point, your spreadsheet should look similar to Figure 3-23.

47

If part of "Quality Scorecard" is NOT underlined with a thick gray line, simply {LEFT-CLICK} the cells necessary to complete the underlining and repeat steps 1 through 5 above.

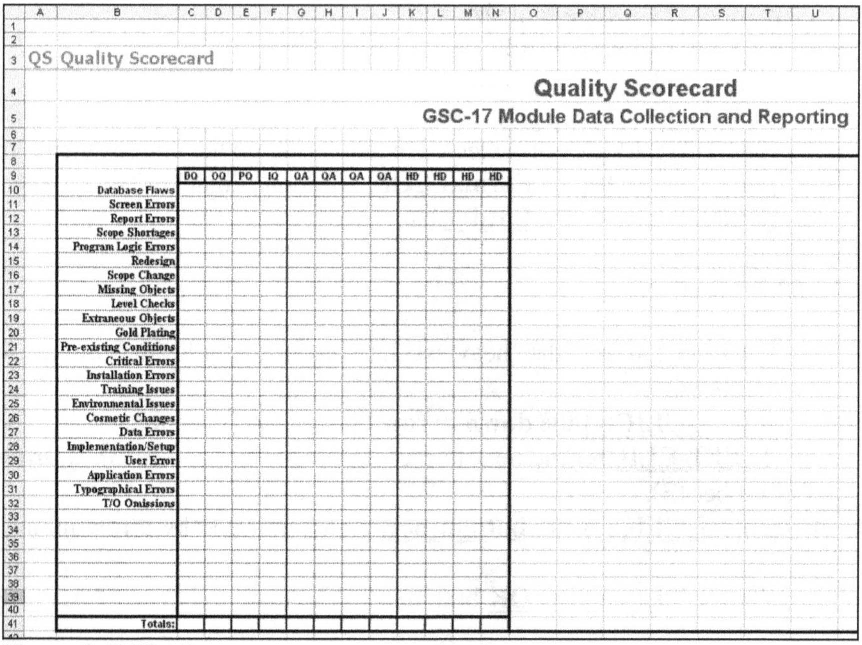

Figure 3-23 Headers

However, we have two more tasks to complete our borders and formatting process.

1. **{LEFT-CLICK}** cell **B6.**
2. **Hold** the **SHIFT** key down.
3. **{LEFT-CLICK}** cell **K6**.

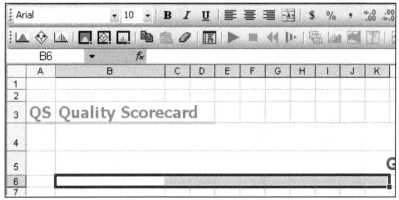

Figure 3-24 Select Cells <u>B6</u> through <u>K6</u>

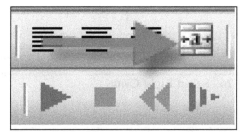

Figure 3-25 - Merge-Center button

4. **{LEFT-CLICK}** the **<u>Merge/Center</u>** button as shown in Figure 3-25.
5. **{RIGHT-CLICK}** the selected area to display the formatting menu.
6. **{LEFT-CLICK}** on **<u>Format Cells...</u>** to display the formatting options.
7. **{LEFT-CLICK}** on the '**Patterns**' tab.
8. **{LEFT-CLICK}** the lightest shade of **cyan** (**light-blue**). (Figure 3-26.)
9. **{LEFT-CLICK}** the **<u>OK</u>** button.

[This will be the <u>Fill</u> tab in Excel 2007.]

49

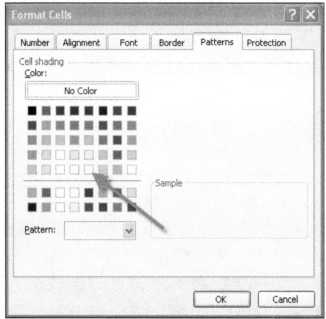

Figure 3-26 - Select Light Cyan

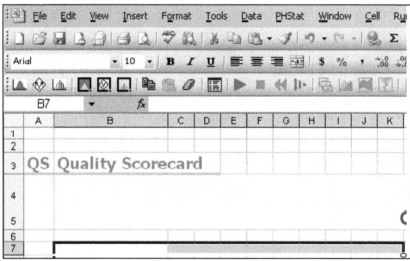

Figure 3-27 Select Cells B7 through K7

Select the cells **B7** through **K7** and repeat the process.

The final formatting process we need to perform is to define the '**Quality**' steps headings.

The first step will be to adjust the row height for row number eight. To do this,

1. **{RIGHT-CLICK}** the number **8** at the far left side of the spreadsheet. (The row label.)

The menu in Figure 3-28 will be displayed.

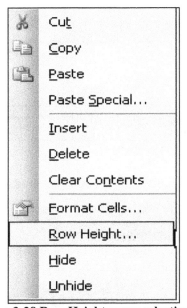

Figure 3-28 <u>Row Height</u> menu selection

2. **{LEFT-CLICK}** **Row-Height...** to display the row height control box as shown in Figure 3-29.

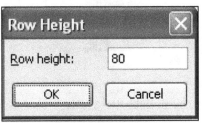

Figure 3-29 <u>Row Height</u> setting

3. Type '**80**' in the **Row Height** box.
4. **{LEFT-CLICK}** the **OK** button.

The height of row number eight will now be dramatically larger than the other rows. See Figure 3-30.

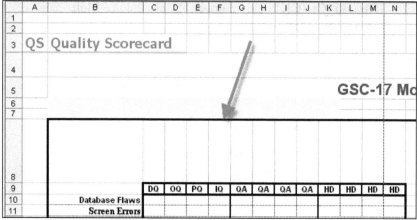

Figure 3-30 Row Height expanded

There are several steps involved in this final heading adjustment:

1. We must change the **font.**
2. We must change the **alignment** of the text.
3. We must change the **direction** of the text.
4. We must set the **color** of the text.

To do this;

    1. **{LEFT-CLICK}** cell **C8**.
    2. **Hold** the **SHIFT** key down.
    3. **{LEFT-CLICK}** cell **N8**.

Figure 3-31 Setting Font, Bold, and Center

Looking at Figure 3-31, and following the arrows left to right;

    4. **{LEFT-CLICK}** the **Times New Roman** font. (You may need to drag the scroll bar downward to find **Times New Roman**.)
    5. **{LEFT-CLICK}** the size to change it to **12**.
    6. **{LEFT-CLICK}** the **Bold** button.

7. {LEFT-CLICK} the **Center** button.

This sets the font and the alignment of the text for the primary headings.

With cells **C8** through **N8** still selected;

1. {RIGHT-CLICK} to display the formatting menu (Figure 3-2).
2. {RIGHT-CLICK} the selected area to display the formatting dialog box.
3. {LEFT-CLICK} the **Alignment** tab.

Looking at Figure 3-32, there are three actions we want to perform:

a. Ensure the text is centered **horizontally** (**1**).
b. Ensure the text is centered **vertically**   (**2**).
c. Adjust the orientation to **45** degrees   (**3**).

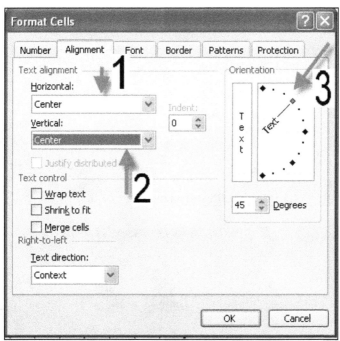

Figure 3-32 Setting Alignment and Orientation

The **Horizontal** alignment (**1**) should be **Center**. If not,
1. {LEFT-CLICK} the **down-arrow** at the right edge of the selection box.
2. {LEFT-CLICK} **Center** from the drop-down list.

The **Vertical** alignment (**2**) should be **Center**. If not,

1. {LEFT-CLICK} the **down-arrow** at the right edge of the selection box.
2. {LEFT-CLICK} **Center** from the drop-down list.

To adjust the orientation (**3**), either

1. Type '**45**' in the **Degrees** edit box, OR
   a. {LEFT-CLICK} the right end of the line extending from the word **Text**.
   b. **Hold** the **left** mouse button down while dragging it to the **45-degree** marker as shown in Figure 3-32.

Next,

1. {LEFT-CLICK} the **Border** tab.
2. {LEFT-CLICK} the next to the heaviest line.
3. {LEFT-CLICK} the **Outline** button.
4. {LEFT-CLICK} the **Inside** button.
5. {LEFT-CLICK} the **OK** button.

The last formatting step is to apply color to the cells. We will work backward, from the right to the left.

1. {LEFT-CLICK} cell **N9**.
2. **Hold** the **SHIFT** key down.
3. {LEFT-CLICK} cell **K8**.
4. {RIGHT-CLICK} to display the options menu.
5. {LEFT-CLICK} **Format Cells...** to display the formatting dialog box.
6. {LEFT-CLICK} the **Patterns** tab.

*[This will be the **Fill** tab in Excel 2007.]*

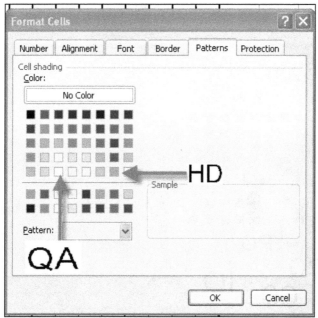

Figure 3-33 HD and QA color settings

Looking at Figure 3-33,

7. **{LEFT-CLICK}** the color box indicated by the '**HD**' arrow (**purple**).
8. **{LEFT-CLICK}** the **OK** button.

1. **{LEFT-CLICK}** cell **J9**.
2. **Hold** the **SHIFT** key down.
3. **{LEFT-CLICK}** cell **G8**
4. **{RIGHT-CLICK}** to display the options menu.
5. **{LEFT-CLICK}** **Format Cells...** to display the formatting dialog box.
6. **{LEFT-CLICK}** the **Patterns** tab. *(The Fill tab for Excel 2007.)*
7. **{LEFT-CLICK}** the color box indicated by the '**QA**' arrow (**yellow**).
8. **{LEFT-CLICK}** the **OK** button.

For the remaining for columns, we will perform a similar process, referencing Figure 3-34.

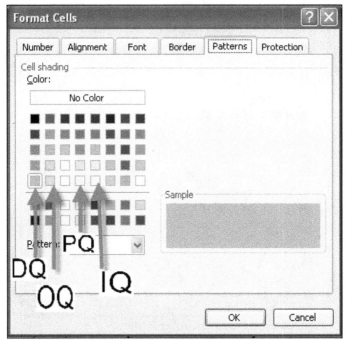

Figure 3-34 Setting DQ - OQ - PQ - IQ colors

1. {LEFT-CLICK} cell **F9**.
2. **Hold** the **SHIFT** key down (or you can use the **CTRL** key for this exercise).
3. {LEFT-CLICK} cell **F8**.
4. {RIGHT-CLICK} to display the options menu.
5. {LEFT-CLICK} **Format Cells…** to display the formatting dialog box.
6. {LEFT-CLICK} the color box indicated by the '**IQ**' arrow (**orange**).
7. {LEFT-CLICK} the '**OK**' button.

Looking at Figure 3-34,

1. {LEFT-CLICK} cell **E9**.
2. **Hold** the **SHIFT** key down.
3. {LEFT-CLICK} cell **E8**.
4. {RIGHT-CLICK} to display the options menu.
5. {LEFT-CLICK} '**Format Cells…**' to display the formatting dialog box.
6. {LEFT-CLICK} the color box indicated by the '**PQ**' arrow (**green**).
7. {LEFT-CLICK} the **OK** button.

Looking at Figure 3-34,

1. **{LEFT-CLICK}** cell **D9**.
2. **Hold** the **SHIFT** key down.
3. **{LEFT-CLICK}** cell **D8**.
4. **{RIGHT-CLICK}** to display the options menu.
5. **{LEFT-CLICK} Format Cells...** to show the format dialog box.
6. **{LEFT-CLICK}** the color box indicated by the '**OQ**' arrow (**light-blue**).
7. **{LEFT-CLICK}** the **OK** button.

Looking at Figure 3-34,

1. **{LEFT-CLICK}** cell **C9**.
2. **Hold** the **SHIFT** key down.
3. **{LEFT-CLICK}** cell **C8**.
4. **{RIGHT-CLICK}** to display the options menu.
5. **{LEFT-CLICK} Format Cells...** to display the formatting dialog box.
6. **{LEFT-CLICK}** the color box indicated by the '**DQ**' arrow (**pink**).
7. **{LEFT-CLICK}** the **OK** button.

Upon completion of these steps, the formatting is finished. However, the orientation of the cells does not appear to be **45-degrees**. To remedy this problem, do the following steps:

1. **{LEFT-CLICK}** cell **C8**.
2. Type '**Project Manager**' and press the **ENTER** key. (The cursor should move to the **right**. The words "**Project Manager**" may appear to print across column **D**, do not worry about this.)
3. Perform the following operations:

Type '**Developer**'	Press the **ENTER** key.
Type '**Team Member**'	Press the **ENTER** key.
Type '**Package Manager**'	Press the **ENTER** key.
Type '**QA Analyst**'	Press the **ENTER** key.
Type '**QA Analyst**'	Press the **ENTER** key.
Type '**QA Analyst**'	Press the **ENTER** key.
Type '**QA Analyst**'	Press the **ENTER** key.
Type '**Support**'	Press the **ENTER** key.
Type '**Support**'	Press the **ENTER** key.
Type '**Support**'	Press the **ENTER** key.
Type '**Support**'	Press the **ENTER** key.

Note that each time you pressed the **ENTER** key, the column header adjusted to a 45-degree orientation. Check your spelling, making any corrections necessary.

NOTE: You may need to adjust the height of row **8**.

Save your work

At this point, the spreadsheet should look similar to Figure 3-35.

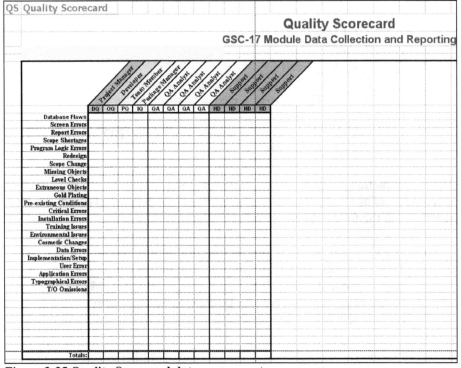

Figure 3-35 Quality Scorecard data components

Chapter 4
Formula

Before we jump into the concept of formula manipulation, we need to perform a bit more formatting of our spreadsheet.

1. **{LEFT-CLICK}** cell **C10**.
2. **Hold** the **SHIFT** key down.
3. **{LEFT-CLICK}** cell **O41**.

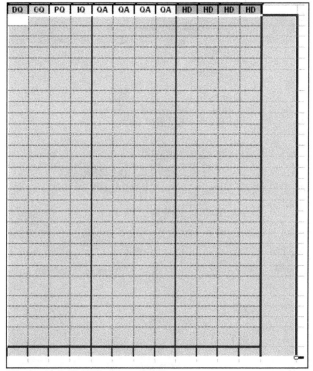

Figure 4-1 Cell Range selection

Since we will be performing mathematical functions on these cells, we need to ensure that they are formatted as numeric fields.

1. **{RIGHT-CLICK}** the selected area to display the **Options** menu.
2. **{LEFT-CLICK}** **Format Cells...** (Figure 4-2).

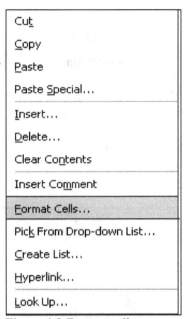

Figure 4-2 Format cells

3. **{LEFT-CLICK}** the **Number** tab.
4. In the **Category** box **{LEFT-CLICK} Number**.
5. In the **Decimal Places** box, change the value to '**0**' (zero). See Figure 4-3.

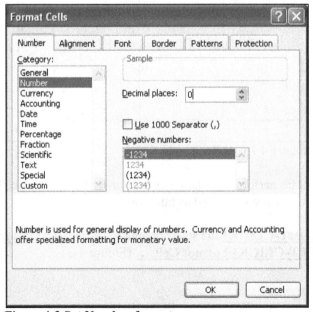

Figure 4-3 Set Number format

6. {LEFT-CLICK} the **OK** button.

Depending upon your spreadsheet settings, your spreadsheet may now look like Figure 4-4.

DO	OO	PO	IO	OA	OA	OA	OA	HD	HD	HD	HD	
0	0	0	0	0	0	0	0	0	0	0	0	0
0	0	0	0	0	0	0	0	0	0	0	0	0
0	0	0	0	0	0	0	0	0	0	0	0	0
0	0	0	0	0	0	0	0	0	0	0	0	0
0	0	0	0	0	0	0	0	0	0	0	0	0
0	0	0	0	0	0	0	0	0	0	0	0	0
0	0	0	0	0	0	0	0	0	0	0	0	0
0	0	0	0	0	0	0	0	0	0	0	0	0
0	0	0	0	0	0	0	0	0	0	0	0	0
0	0	0	0	0	0	0	0	0	0	0	0	0
0	0	0	0	0	0	0	0	0	0	0	0	0
0	0	0	0	0	0	0	0	0	0	0	0	0
0	0	0	0	0	0	0	0	0	0	0	0	0
0	0	0	0	0	0	0	0	0	0	0	0	0
0	0	0	0	0	0	0	0	0	0	0	0	0
0	0	0	0	0	0	0	0	0	0	0	0	0
0	0	0	0	0	0	0	0	0	0	0	0	0
0	0	0	0	0	0	0	0	0	0	0	0	0
0	0	0	0	0	0	0	0	0	0	0	0	0
0	0	0	0	0	0	0	0	0	0	0	0	0
0	0	0	0	0	0	0	0	0	0	0	0	0
0	0	0	0	0	0	0	0	0	0	0	0	0
0	0	0	0	0	0	0	0	0	0	0	0	0
0	0	0	0	0	0	0	0	0	0	0	0	0
0	0	0	0	0	0	0	0	0	0	0	0	0
0	0	0	0	0	0	0	0	0	0	0	0	0
0	0	0	0	0	0	0	0	0	0	0	0	0
0	0	0	0	0	0	0	0	0	0	0	0	0
0	0	0	0	0	0	0	0	0	0	0	0	0
0	0	0	0	0	0	0	0	0	0	0	0	0
0	0	0	0	0	0	0	0	0	0	0	0	0

Figure 4-4 Zero Values displayed

While this is not a big problem, the zeros make the spreadsheet look messy and add unnecessary 'noise' to our document. Hiding the zero values is a simple process.

Figure 4-5 <u>Tools</u> - <u>Options</u> selection

1. **{LEFT-CLICK}** the **Options** menu selection to display the **Options** Dialog box as shown in Figure 4-6.
2. **{LEFT-CLICK}** the **View** tab.

62

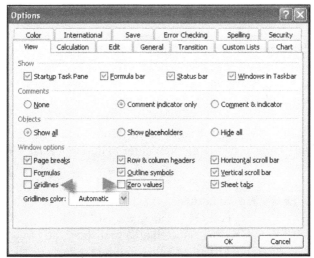
Figure 4-6 Zero Values checkbox

3. Make sure the **Zero Value's** checkbox is not checked (there should not be a 'check mark' in this box.)
4. If the **Zero Values** checkbox has a 'check mark' in it,
    a. **{LEFT-CLICK}** the **Zero Values** checkbox to 'uncheck' it.
5. **{LEFT-CLICK}** the **OK** button.

[For Excel 2007,
    A. {LEFT-CLICK} the LOGO in the upper left corner.
    B. {LEFT-CLICK} the EXCEL OPTIONS button.
    C. {LEFT-CLICK} the ADVANCED button.
    D. {LEFT-CLICK} the SHOW A ZERO IN CELLS THAT HAVE A ZERO VALUE to un-check it.
        a. You may need to scroll down to find it.
    E. {LEFT-CLICK} the OK button.]

With the same selection range, looking at Figure 4-7:

1. **{LEFT-CLICK}** the **Bold** button on the tool bar at the top of the spreadsheet.
2. **{LEFT-CLICK}** the **Center** button on the tool bar at the top of the spreadsheet.

Figure 4-7 Bold and Center buttons

This will cause the numbers entered in these cells to be bolded and centered within the cell margins.

Note that the **Font, Style** and **Size** should be (**Arial, Regular, 10**) for all cells in this selection. (Make these adjustments if necessary.)

Next we need to make a slight adjustment to the formatting for the cells in Column **O**. We want to change the font color to de-emphasize these values.

1. **{LEFT-CLICK}** cell **O9**.
2. **Hold** the **SHIFT** key down.
3. **{LEFT-CLICK}** cell **O41**. The range will be highlighted.
4. **{RIGHT-CLICK}** the selected area to display the **Options** menu.
5. **{LEFT-CLICK}** **Format Cells...** (Figure 4-2).

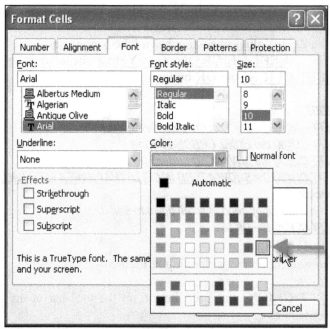

Figure 4-8 Select Gray font

6. **{LEFT-CLICK}** the **Font** tab.
7. **{LEFT-CLICK}** the **down-arrow** on the **Color** selection box to display the color palette.
8. **{LEFT-CLICK}** the **lightest gray** (the fourth box from the top).
9. **{LEFT-CLICK}** the **OK** button.

With the basic formatting completed, we can start entering our formula.

First, we want to add everything from column **C** through column **N** for rows **10** through **41**. This sounds like a lot of work, but it can be performed with a few mouse clicks.

Figure 4-9 Autosum button

1. **{LEFT-CLICK}** cell **O10**.
2. **{LEFT-CLICK}** the **Autosum** button (Figure 4-9). The **Autosum** button has the uppercase sigma character ($\sum$) on it.

*[This will be the **Formulas** tab in Excel 2007.]*

3. **{LEFT-CLICK}** cell **N10**.
4. **Hold** the **SHIFT** key down.
5. **{LEFT-CLICK}** cell **C10**.
6. Press the **ENTER** key.
7. **{LEFT-CLICK}** cell **O10**.

Note that the formula bar now has '**=SUM(C10:N10)**' displayed. The equal sign (=) at the beginning of the formula tells us that the contents of the current cell (**O10**) is equal to the result of the formula. What this formula tells us is that we are adding (Summation, or **SUM**) everything between cells **C10** and cell **N10**.

This process can be repeated for each row OR we can do it the quick way. To quickly replicate this formula in the remaining rows,

1. **{LEFT-CLICK}** cell **O10**.
2. **Hold** the **CTRL** key down and press the C key.
3. Release both keys.
4. **{LEFT-CLICK}** cell **O11**.
5. **Hold** the **SHIFT** key down,
6. **{LEFT-CLICK}** cell **O41**.
7. **{RIGHT-CLICK}** the selected area to display an **Options** menu as shown in Figure 4-10.

65

8. {LEFT-CLICK} the **Paste Special...** menu option to display the **Paste Special** dialogue box as shown in Figure 4-11.

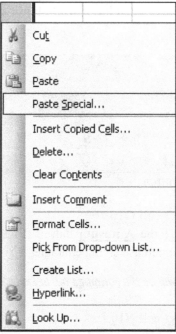

Figure 4-10 Paste Special menu

1. **{LEFT-CLICK} Formulas**.
2. **{LEFT-CLICK}** the **OK** button.

Note: you could also use the **CTRL-V** (Hold the **CTRL** key down while pressing the **V** key) combination to do the same thing, but it copies everything and can sometimes result in unexpected results.

Press the **ESC** key to clear the selection box (the dashed lines around cell **C10**).

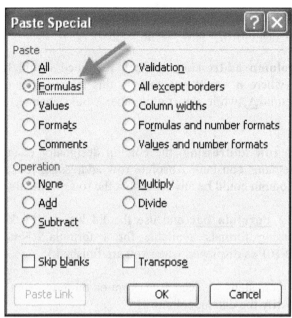
Figure 4-11 **Paste Special** dialogue box

This process has copied the formula from cell **O10** to every cell between cell **O11** and **O41**.

If you click in any cell in Column **O**, the **Formula bar** will display a different formula.

At this time, we will take a brief moment to discuss cell addressing in Excel. There are two common forms of addressing cells; **Relative** and **Absolute**. The default is **Relative addressing**, in which each cell is referenced by its unique column and row designation (column **O**, row **30**).

Note that as you **{LEFT-CLICK}** each row in column **O**, starting with cell **O10** and ending with **O41**, the left side of the **Formula bar** will reflect the same column (**O**) with a row number that corresponds to the actual row.

The second form of addressing will be used later in the book. It is **Absolute addressing**, in which a specific cell is always used, regardless of any copying functions. **Absolute addressing** has a format of **$A$3**.

The dollar sign ($) indicates **Absolute addressing** and applies to the column and row levels. Therefore, **$A** always refers to column **A**. The **$3** always refers to row **3**. As such **$A$3** always refers to cell **A3**.

Two interesting variants to absolute addressing is the absolute column addressing and absolute row addressing.

In **absolute column addressing**, the cell reference would look like **$A1** through **$An** (where **n** = any number). In this instance the column would always be column **A**, while the row number would change, relative to the actual row.

With **absolute row addressing**, the column designator changes while the row number remains constant. Absolute row addressing looks like **A$3**. In this case, the column could be any letter, but the row would always be **3**.

Note: Click the **Formula bar** and use the **F4** key to 'cycle' through the various addressing formats available for a formula. (Note: make sure '=SUM(C10:N10)' is displayed when you are finished.)

There are two more steps we need to perform on our cross-foot column. First, we will **left-justify** the data in column **O**.

1. **{LEFT-CLICK}** cell **O10**.
2. **Hold** the **SHIFT** key down.
3. **{LEFT-CLICK}** cell **O41**.
4. **{RIGHT-CLICK}** the selected area to display the **Format Cells** menu (Figure 4-2).
5. **{LEFT-CLICK} Format Cells** to display the formatting options screen.
6. **{LEFT-CLICK}** the **Alignment** tab.
7. Under **Text Alignment**, **{LEFT-CLICK}** the **down-arrow** to the right of the **Horizontal** drop-down box.
8. **{LEFT-CLICK}** the **Left (indent)** alignment selection.
9. **{LEFT-CLICK}** the **OK** button.

Our next step is to provide the formula for the **Totals** row. To do this,

10. **{LEFT-CLICK}** cell **C41**.
11. **{LEFT-CLICK}** the **Autosum** button (Figure 4-9). The **Autosum** button has the uppercase sigma character ($\sum$) on it.
12. **{LEFT-CLICK}** cell **C10**.
13. **Hold** the **SHIFT** key down.
14. **{LEFT-CLICK}** cell **C40**.
15. Press the **ENTER** key.
16. **{LEFT-CLICK}** cell **C41** and note that the **Formula bar** now has '=SUM(C10:C40)' displayed. This formula tells us that cell **C41** is equal to the **SUM** of everything from cell **C10** through cell **C40**.

68

To quickly replicate this formula in the remaining rows:

1. **{LEFT-CLICK}** cell **C41**.
2. **Hold** the **CTRL** key down and press the C key.
3. Release both keys.
4. **{LEFT-CLICK}** cell **D41**.
5. **Hold** the **SHIFT** key down.
6. **{LEFT-CLICK}** cell **N41**.
7. **{RIGHT-CLICK}** the selected area to display an **Options** menu as shown in Figure 4-10.
8. **{LEFT-CLICK}** the **Paste Special...** menu option to display the **Paste Special** dialogue box as shown in Figure 4-11.
9. **{LEFT-CLICK}** **Formulas**.
10. **{LEFT-CLICK}** the **OK** button.
11. Press the **ESC** key to clear the selection.

The formula in cell **C41** has been copied into cells **D41** through **N41**. Again, to verify this, simply use the **TAB** key to progress through cells **D41** to **N41**, noting that the contents of the **Formula bar** changes with each press of the **TAB** key.

Also note that the formula uses **relative addressing**.

To do a quick test drive, enter some numbers in the cells between **C10** and **N40**. After each entry, note the effects in row **41** and column **O**. Each time a number is added to a row, the row total (column **O**) changes to reflect the new sum. If the number is deleted, the sum is reduced.

Similarly any entry in a column updates the column totals located in row **41**.

There are several ways to remove the numbers from our grid (cells **C10** through **N40**).

1. **{LEFT-CLICK}** a cell with a number to be removed and press the **BACKSPACE** key.
2. **{LEFT-CLICK}** a cell with a number to be removed and press the **DELETE** or **DEL** key.
3. **{LEFT-CLICK}** a cell with a number to be removed and press the **SPACE** key. (This is not advisable, since it may cause issues with some number formats.)
4. Clear the grid all at one time.
   a. **{LEFT-CLICK}** cell **C10**.
   b. **Hold** the **SHIFT** key down.

c. **{LEFT-CLICK}** cell **N40**.
d. **{RIGHT-CLICK}** the selected area to display the '**Options**' Menu.
e. **{LEFT-CLICK}** on **Clear Contents**. (Figure 4-12).
f. Press the **ESC** key to clear the selection.

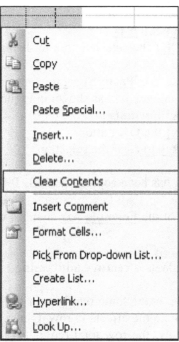

Figure 4-12 Clear Contents

Save your work.

There are a couple of 'housekeeping tasks we can do to make our work a little easier.

How to make the entire working area visible without having to use the scroll bar at the bottom of the spreadsheet:

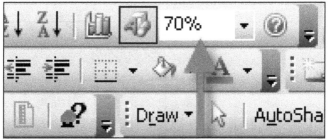

Figure 4-13 Setting <u>Viewing Size</u>

As shown in Figure 4-13, at the top of the screen, is a box with a percentage in it (probably 100%). To adjust the **<u>Viewing Size</u>** so that the entire working area is displayed, type '**70**' in this box and press the **ENTER** key. The spreadsheet will shrink proportionally.

[In Excel 2007, there is an adjustment at the lower right corner.]

Depending upon your screen and eyesight, you may adjust this as necessary to provide the best working area.

(Do not be concerned if some of the text in column **<u>B</u>** extends beyond the border.)

How to set page breaks:

If you look closely at your spreadsheet, you may see two (or more) dotted lines. These indicate where the spreadsheet will start a new page when printing. (Figure 4-14).

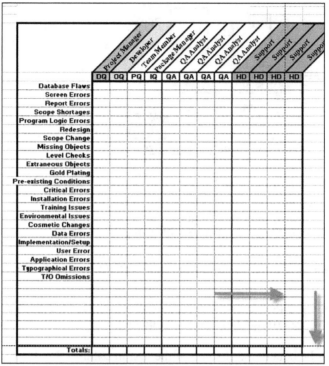

Figure 4-14 **Page Break** indicators

To control how the printed report will be defined;

1. {LEFT-CLICK} on the **View** menu item (Figure 4-15).
2. {LEFT-CLICK} **Page Break Preview**.

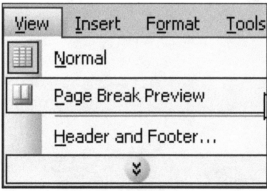

Figure 4-15 **Page Break Review**

Figure 4-16 illustrates the **Page Break Preview**. From this screen, it is a simple matter to adjust the pagination for the spreadsheet.

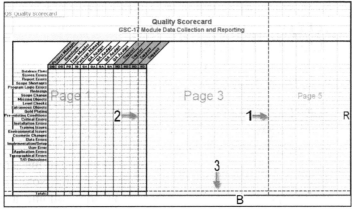

Figure 4-16 Page Break view

1. **{LEFT-CLICK}** the right dashed line (**1**).
2. **Hold** the **left** mouse button down while dragging the cursor to the **right** until reaching the line indicated by the letter '**R**'.
3. Release the mouse button.
4. Repeat the process with the left dashed line (if it is still visible). (It may have turned solid.)
5. If the bottom dashed line is still visible,
   a. **{LEFT-CLICK}** the bottom dashed line.
   b. **Hold** the left mouse button down while dragging the cursor **downward** to the line marked with the letter '**B**'.

Note that some or all of the lines will self-adjust as you drag the first or second lines.

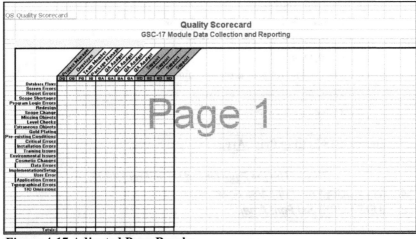

Figure 4-17 Adjusted <u>Page Breaks</u>

73

When there are no more dashed lines visible,
1. {LEFT-CLICK} on the **View** menu item (Figure 4-14).
2. {LEFT-CLICK} **Normal**.

How to define the print area:

1. {LEFT-CLICK} cell **A1**.
2. **Hold** the **SHIFT** key down.
3. {LEFT-CLICK} cell **AC41**.
4. {LEFT-CLICK} the **File** menu item at the top of the screen.
5. {LEFT-CLICK} the **Print Area** menu option. (Note: If the **File** menu option has a **down-arrow** at the bottom, it may be necessary to {LEFT-CLICK} the **down-arrow** to display the full menu.)
6. {LEFT-CLICK} the **Set Print Area** option.

Figure 4-18 Setting Print Area

*[This will be the **Page Layout** tab in Excel 2007.*
A. *{LEFT-CLICK} the **Print Area** down-arrow.*
B. *{LEFT-CLICK} **Set Print Area**].*

Define the print layout.

With the **Print Area** defined, setting the printer layout is an easy task.

1. **{LEFT-CLICK}** the **File** menu item at the top of the screen.
2. **{LEFT-CLICK}** on **Page Setup**. A dialogue box similar to Figure 4-19 will display.
3. **{LEFT-CLICK}** on the **Page** tab.

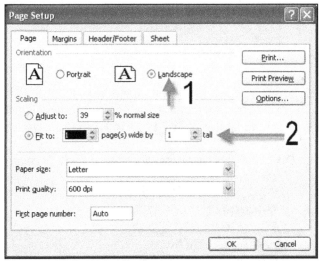

Figure 4-19 Set <u>Print Layout</u>

4. **{LEFT-CLICK}** the **Landscape** radio button.
5. **{LEFT-CLICK}** **Fit to** and make sure the pages **wide** and **tall** are both set to **1**.
6. **{LEFT-CLICK}** the **OK** button.
7. **{LEFT-CLICK}** the **File** menu item at the top of the screen and **{LEFT-CLICK}** on **Print Preview** (See Figure 4-20).

*[This will be the **Page Layout** tab in Excel 2007.*
A.   *{LEFT-CLICK} the **Orientation** down-arrow.*
B.   *{LEFT-CLICK} **Landscape**.*
C.   *{LEFT-CLICK} the **Width** down-arrow.*
D.   *{LEFT-CLICK} **1 Page**.*
E.   *{LEFT-CLICK} the **Height** down-arrow.*
F.   *{LEFT-CLICK} **1 Page**].*

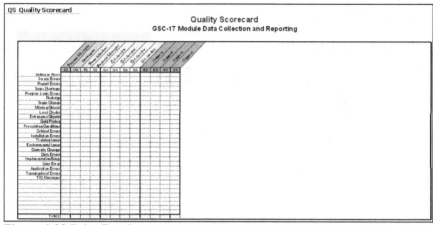

Figure 4-20 <u>Print Preview</u>

Note that your **Print Preview** should include the footer, which I omitted from Figure 4-20 for readability. **{LEFT-CLICK}** the **Close** button.

> *[Note: in Excel 2007, the Footer may have gotten 'lost'. To correct this:*
> **A.** *From the **PRINT PREVIEW** SCREEN:*
> **B.** *{LEFT-CLICK} the **PAGE SETUP** button.*
> **C.** *{LEFT-CLICK} **CUSTOM FOOTER**.*
> **D.** *{LEFT-CLICK} the **LEFT SECTION**.*
> **E.** ***LEFT-CLICK** the **FILE** button.*
> **F.** *{LEFT-CLICK} the **LEFT SECTION**.*
> **G.** *{LEFT-CLICK} the **DATE** button.*
> **H.** *Press the **SPACE** key two times.*
> **I.** *{LEFT-CLICK} the **TIME** button.*
> **J.** *{DOUBLE-CLICK} '&[PATH]&[FILE].*
> **K.** *{LEFT-CLICK} the **FONT** button.*
> > **a.** *Select **ARIAL**.*
> > **b.** *Select **SIZE 8**.*
> **L.** *{DOUBLE-CLICK} '&[DATE]&[TIME].*
> **M.** *{LEFT-CLICK} the **FONT** button.*
> > **a.** *Select **ARIAL**.*
> > **b.** *Select **SIZE 8**.*
> **N.** *{LEFT-CLICK} the **OK** button.*
> **O.** *{LEFT-CLICK} the **OK** button.]*

<u>Save your work.</u>

Chapter 5

Graphing

Now that the basic data components of the spreadsheet have been defined, we can begin to develop a chart that will dynamically reflect our data in a high-impact graphical format.

Figure 5-1 <u>Chart Wizard</u> icon

1. At the top of the screen, locate the chart wizard icon as illustrated in Figure 5-1.
2. **{LEFT-CLICK}** the **Chart Wizard** icon to display the screen shown in Figure 5-2.

*[This will be the <u>**Insert**</u> tab in Excel 2007.*
*A.   **{LEFT-CLICK}** the <u>**Area**</u> down-arrow].*

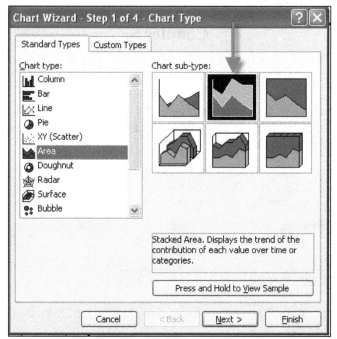

Figure 5-2 <u>Chart Type</u> selection

1. Make sure the **<u>Standard Types</u>** tab is selected.
2. **{LEFT-CLICK}** **<u>Area</u>** to display the six area graphs available.
3. **{LEFT-CLICK}** the middle sub-chart on the top row to the right of the **<u>Chart Type</u>** selection box.
4. **{LEFT-CLICK}** the **<u>Next</u>** button to begin building the chart.

Figure 5-3 will display to allow the selection of the data range to be used for our graph,

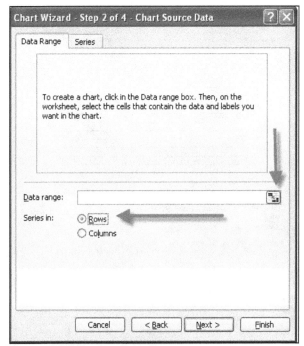

Figure 5-3 Selecting Data Range

To select the **Data Range**:
1. **{LEFT-CLICK}** the **Rows** radio button,
2. **{LEFT-CLICK}** the **Data Range** Selection Box.
3. **{LEFT-CLICK}** cell **C41**.
4. **Hold** the **SHIFT** key down.
5. **{LEFT-CLICK}** cell **N41**. (The selected area should be similar to Figures 5-4 and 5-5.)
6. **{LEFT-CLICK}** the **Next** button.

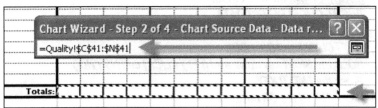

Figure 5-4 Data Range selection

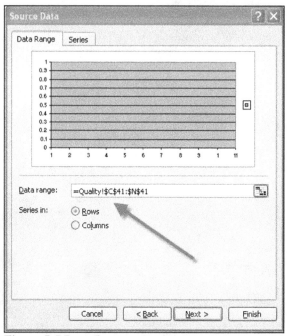

Figure 5-5 <u>Data Range</u> selection

[in Excel 2007 ,
 A. *{LEFT-CLICK} the chart area.*
 B. *{RIGHT-CLICK} the chart area.*
 C. *{RIGHT-CLICK} SELECT DATA.*
 D. *{LEFT CLICK} the CHART DATA RANGE selection box.*
 E. *{LEFT CLICK} cell C41.*
 F. *HOLD the SHIFT key down.*
 G. *{LEFT CLICK} cell N41.*
 H. *Press the ENTER key.*
 I. *{LEFT CLICK} the chart area.*
 J. *{RIGHT-CLICK} the chart area.*
 K. *{RIGHT-CLICK} SELECT DATA.*
 L. *{LEFT CLICK} the HORIZONTAL AXIS LABEL EDIT' button.*
 M. *{LEFT CLICK} cell C9 ('DQ')*
 N. *HOLD the SHIFT key down and {LEFT CLICK} cell N9 ('HD').*
 O. *Press the ENTER KEY.*
 P. *{LEFT CLICK} the OK button.*
 Q. *{LEFT CLICK} the Legend SERIES 1.*
 R. *Press the DEL key.]*

80

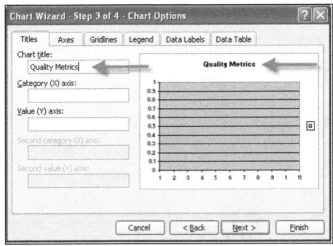

Figure 5-6 Defining Chart Title

After left-clicking the **Next** button, Figure 5-6 will allow us to provide a **Chart Title**.

1. **{LEFT-CLICK}** the **Titles** tab.
2. In the **Chart Title** box, type '**Quality Metrics**'.
3. **{RIGHT-CLICK}** the title to display a **Font** dialogue box.
4. **{LEFT-CLICK} Arial** font.
5. Change the **Size** to '**20**'.
6. **{LEFT-CLICK}** the **Bold** button.
7. **{LEFT-CLICK}** the Chart area.

[In Excel 2007

    A. *{LEFT-CLICK} the Chart area.*
    B. *{LEFT-CLICK} the Layout tab at the top of the screen.*
    C. *{LEFT-CLICK} the Chart Title down-arrow button.*
    D. *LEFT-CLICK} Above Chart..*
    E. *In the CHART TITLE box in the chart box area, type 'QUALITY METRICS' (Without the single quotes).*
    F. *You may need to use the DEL key to remove 'CHART TITLE'.*
    G. *{RIGHT-CLICK} the title to display a Font dialogue box.*
    H. *Select Arial font.*
    I. *Change the size to '20'.*
    J. *{LEFT-CLICK} the Bold button.*
    K. *{LEFT-CLICK} the Chart area.]*

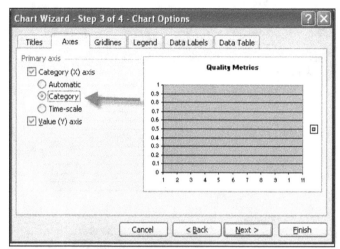

Figure 5-7 Axis Definition

1. **{LEFT-CLICK}** the **Axis** tab.
2. **{LEFT-CLICK}** the **Category** radio button as shown in Figure 5-7.

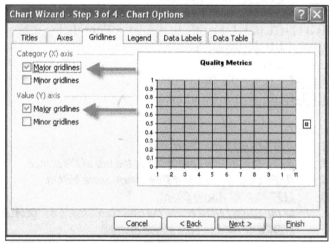

Figure 5-8 Gridline Definition

1. **{LEFT-CLICK}** the **Gridlines** tab.
2. **{LEFT-CLICK}** the **Major Gridlines** check boxes for the **X** and **Y** axis as shown in Figure 5-8.

[In Excel 2007

    A. **{LEFT-CLICK}** *the horizontal axis.*
    B. **{RIGHT-CLICK}** *the horizontal axis.*
    C. **{LEFT-CLICK} add major gridlines.]*

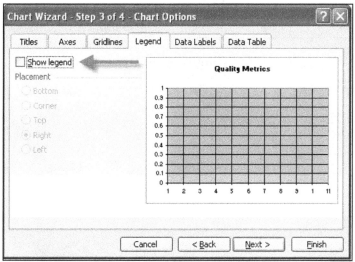

Figure 5-9 Legend suppression

We do not want a legend for our graph.

1. **{LEFT-CLICK}** the **Legend** tab.
2. **{LEFT-CLICK}** the **Show Legend** check box to '**unselect**' the legend as shown in Figure 5-9. (The **Show Legend** check box should be unchecked.)

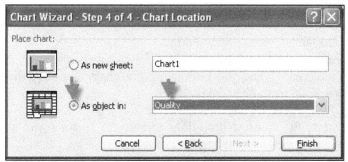

Figure 5-10 Chart placement

The last step in the chart wizard is to place the chart on the spreadsheet. We want this chart to be a part of the **Quality** tab in our spreadsheet (The main tab we have been working on.)

Looking at Figure 5-10,

1. **{LEFT-CLICK}** the **As object in** radio button and make sure the box to the right says '**Quality**'.
2. **{LEFT-CLICK}** the **Finish** button.

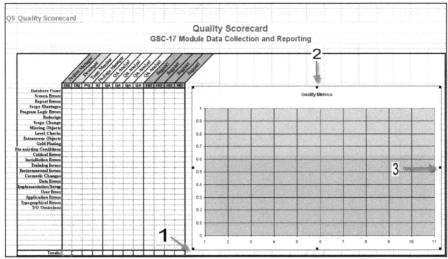

Figure 5-11 Adjusting Chart location

The chart will be placed in the work area on our main tab (**Quality**). Do not be alarmed if the chart 'overlays' our prior work; it is a simple matter to adjust. Looking at Figure 5-11,

1. **{LEFT-CLICK}** any of the 'white space' in the chart.

[In Excel 2007, {LEFT-CLICK} the chart border.]

2. **Hold** the left mouse button down.
3. Drag the chart until the left side of the chart is resting in the middle of column **O** and the bottom of the chart is resting on the line separating rows **40** and **41**.
4. **{LEFT-CLICK}** the black box at the top of the chart and while holding the mouse button down, move the cursor **upward** until the top of the chart is in the middle of row **9**.

[In Excel 2007, the black boxes are replaced with 3 or 4 dots (...).]

5. **{LEFT-CLICK}** the black box at the right of the chart and while holding the mouse button down, move the cursor to the **right** until the right edge of the chart is almost touching the heavy border line.

With the chart properly positioned, we can now make it more presentable.

84

First, we will adjust the quality of the gridlines in the chart. In their current form, they are distracting. We will solve this problem by adjusting the style and color of the chart gridlines.

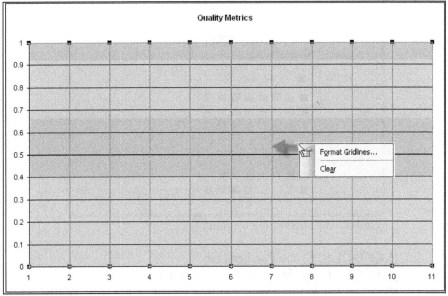

Figure 5-12 Formatting Gridlines

1. **{RIGHT-CLICK}** one of the **vertical** (running top to bottom) grid lines to display the **Format Gridlines** menu option.
2. **{LEFT-CLICK} Format Gridlines** option to display the formatting screen. (Figure 5-13)

[In Excel 2007,
   A.   {RIGHT-CLICK} a __vertical__ gridline.
   B.   {LEFT-CLICK} the __Format Gridlines__ menu option.
   C.   {LEFT-CLICK} the __LINE STYLE__ button.
   D.   {LEFT-CLICK} the __DASH TYPE__ down-arrow.
   E.   {LEFT-CLICK} the round dot dash type (second from the top).
   F.   {LEFT-CLICK} the __LINE COLOR__ button.
   G.   {LEFT-CLICK} the __COLOR__ down-arrow.
   H.   {LEFT-CLICK} the darkest shade of __gray__ (Second from the bottom).
   I.   {LEFT-CLICK} the __CLOSE__ button.]

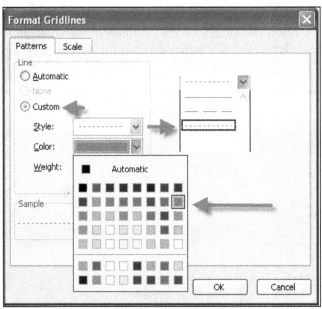

Figure 5-13 Formatting options

3. **{LEFT-CLICK}** the **Patterns** tab.
4. **{LEFT-CLICK}** the **Custom** radio button.
5. **{LEFT-CLICK}** the **down-arrow** on the right side of the **Style** selection box.
6. **{LEFT-CLICK}** the dashed line.
7. **{LEFT-CLICK}** the **down-arrow** on the right side of the **Color** selection box.
8. From the color palette, **{LEFT-CLICK}** the heaviest **gray** (Second from the top)
9. **{LEFT-CLICK}** the **OK** button.

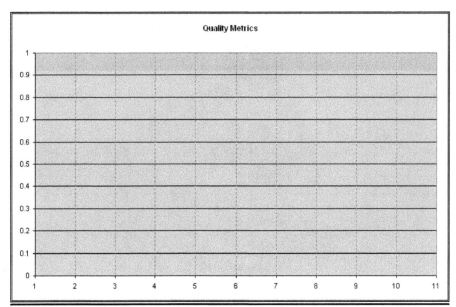

Figure 5-14 Dashed <u>Vertical</u> gridlines

The chart should look similar to Figure 5-14.

Next, we need to define the **<u>X</u>** (horizontal) and **<u>Y</u>** (Vertical) Axes. We will begin with the X-Axis.

Figure 5-15 Source Data menu

1. **{RIGHT-CLICK}** on the white area of the chart to display the formatting pop-up menu. (Figure 5-16).

   [In Excel 2007, (completed in a previous step):
   A. {LEFT-CLICK} the chart area.
   B. {RIGHT-CLICK} the chart area.
   C. {LEFT-CLICK} Select Data.
   D. {LEFT-CLICK} the Horizontal Axis Labels EDIT -button.
   E. {LEFT-CLICK} C9 ('DO').
   F. HOLD the SHIFT key DOWN.
   G. {LEFT-CLICK} N9 ('HD').
   H. {LEFT-CLICK} the OK button]

2. **{LEFT-CLICK}** on **Source Data** to display the series selection screen. (Figure 5-16)

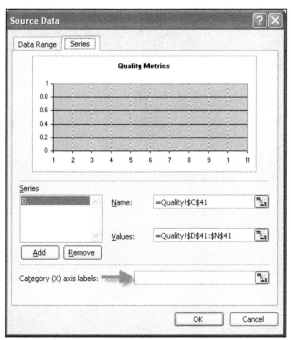
Figure 5-16 X-Axis Labels

3. **{LEFT-CLICK}** the **Series** tab.
4. **{LEFT-CLICK}** in the **Category (X) axis labels** drop down box.

89

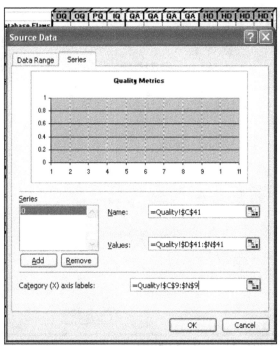

Figure 5-17 X-Axis Label selection

5. **{LEFT-CLICK}** cell **C9**.
6. **Hold** the **SHIFT** key down.
7. **{LEFT-CLICK}** cell **N9**.
8. **{LEFT-CLICK}** the **OK** button.

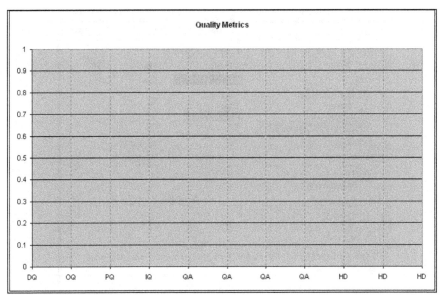

Figure 5-18 X-Axis

Note in Figure 5-18 that the labels for the X-Axis now reflect the twelve category columns we defined for our data elements. However, the labels are somewhat understated, so we will adjust the font.

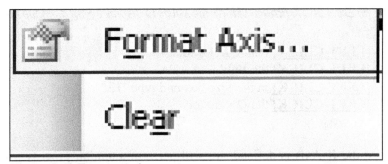

Figure 5-19 Format Axis

{**RIGHT-CLICK**} one of the labels on the X-Axis to display the pop-up menu in Figure 5-19.

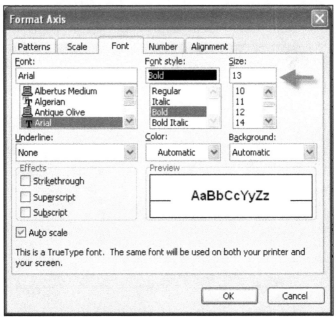

Figure 5-20 Setting Axis font

Looking at Figure 5-20, **{LEFT-CLICK}** the '**Font**' tab.

*[In Excel 2007, **{RIGHT-CLICK}** the X-Axis to display a **Font** dialogue box.]*

1. **{LEFT-CLICK}** on the **Arial** font.
2. **{LEFT-CLICK}** the **Bold** font style.
3. **{LEFT-CLICK}** in the **Size** box and type '**13**'.
4. **{LEFT-CLICK}** the **OK** button.

Now that the X-Axis is defined, we will perform a similar process with the Y-Axis.

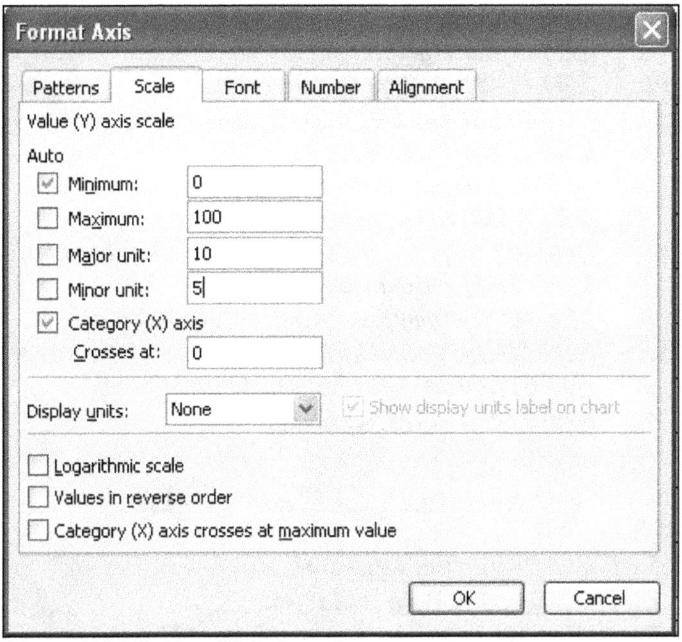

Figure 5-21 Setting Y-Axis scale

{**RIGHT-CLICK**} one of the labels on the Y-Axis to display the pop-up menu in Figure 5-21.

1. {**LEFT-CLICK**} the **Scale** tab.
2. {**LEFT-CLICK**} the **Minimum** box.
3. Type '**0**'.

4. {**LEFT-CLICK**} the **Maximum** box.
5. Type '**100**'.

6. {**LEFT-CLICK**} the **Major Unit** box.
7. Type '**10**'.

8. {**LEFT-CLICK**} the **Minor Unit** box.
9. Type '**5**'.

10. {**LEFT-CLICK**} the **Font** Tab.

You can set these values to anything that meets your needs. The values used in this exercise are adequate for our presentation needs.

[In Excel 2007,
    A.   {LEFT-CLICK} the Y-Axis.

B.   *{RIGHT-CLICK} the Y-Axis to display the options menu.*
C.   *{LEFT-CLICK} FORMAT AXIS.*
D.   *{LEFT-CLICK} the AXIS Options button.*
E.   *{LEFT-CLICK} four fixed radio buttons.*
F.   *{LEFT-CLICK} the top fixed box.*
G.   *Type '0'. (You may need to delete the existing value.)*
H.   *{LEFT-CLICK} the second fixed box.*
I.   *Type '100'. (You may need to delete the existing value.)*
J.   *{LEFT-CLICK} the third fixed box.*
K.   *Type '10'. (You may need to delete the existing value.)*
L.   *{LEFT-CLICK} the bottom fixed box.*
M.   *Type '5'. (You may need to delete the existing value.)*
N.   *{LEFT-CLICK} the CLOSE button.*

Looking at Figure 5-21, **{LEFT-CLICK}** on the **Font** tab.

1.   **{LEFT-CLICK}** on the **Arial** font.
2.   **{LEFT-CLICK}** the **Bold** font style.
3.   **{LEFT-CLICK}** in the size box and type '**13**'.
4.   **{LEFT-CLICK}** the **OK** button.

[In Excel 2007,
   A.   *{RIGHT-CLICK} the Y-Axis to display the options menu.*
   B.   *{LEFT-CLICK} Font.*
   C.   *{LEFT-CLICK} the Font down-arrow button.*
   D.   *{LEFT-CLICK} ARIAL.*
   E.   *{LEFT-CLICK} the Font Style down-arrow button.*
   F.   *{LEFT-CLICK} BOLD.*
   G.   *{LEFT-CLICK} SIZE selection box.*
   H.   *Type 13.*
   I.   *{LEFT-CLICK} the OK button.*

At this point, much of the chart definition work is complete. However, there is a final point of presentation to make. Our spreadsheet has gridlines and zero values that clutter up its presentation quality.

To solve this problem,

{LEFT-CLICK} on the **Tools** menu item at the top of the screen as shown in Figure 5-22.

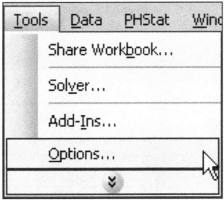

Figure 5-22 Options menu selection

When you {LEFT-CLICK} Options, a display similar to Figure 5-23 will be presented.

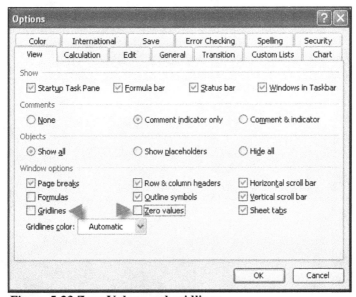

Figure 5-23 Zero Values and gridlines

1. {LEFT-CLICK} the **Gridlines** box to 'uncheck' it.
2. {LEFT-CLICK} the **Zero Values** box to 'uncheck' it.
3. {LEFT-CLICK} the **OK** button.

[For Excel 2007,

    *A.   {LEFT-CLICK} the **logo** in the upper left corner.*
    *B.   {LEFT-CLICK} the **Excel Options** button.*
    *C.   {LEFT-CLICK} the **Advanced** button.*
    *D.   Scroll down to **Display options for this worksheet**.*

95

The spreadsheet should look similar to Figure 5-24. Note that the gridlines behind our working area are no longer visible on the spreadsheet.

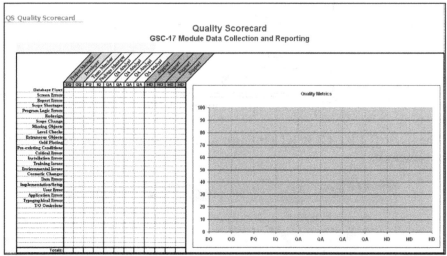

Figure 5-24 Chapter Five chart

Save your work.

Chapter 6

Testing the Score Card

We have completed the spreadsheet and have a Quality Score Card ready for testing.

Top do this, we will begin by typing '**10**' in cell **C10** and press the **ENTER** key. Note that the number '**10**' appeared in cell **O10** (between the last '**HD**' and the chart). However, nothing significant appears to have happened on the chart itself.

For a temporary test, we will add another formula to the spreadsheet. (We will remove it shortly.)

1. {**LEFT-CLICK**} cell **A10**.
2. {**LEFT-CLICK**} the formula bar at the top of the screen
3. Type '=' (Without the quote marks).
4. {**LEFT-CLICK**} cell **O10**.
5. Type '/' (Without the quote marks).
6. {**LEFT-CLICK**} cell **O41**.
7. Press the **ENTER** key.
8. The number '**1**' should be visible in cell **A10**.

Now, we will set the format for column **A**.

1. {**LEFT-CLICK**} On cell **A10**.
2. **Hold** the **SHIFT** key down.
3. {**LEFT-CLICK**} On cell **A41**.
4. {**LEFT-CLICK**} The **Center** button at the top of the screen.
5. {**RIGHT-CLICK**} the selected area to display the pop-up menu.
6. {**LEFT-CLICK**} **Format Cells** to display the **Format Cells** dialogue box as shown in Figure 6-1.

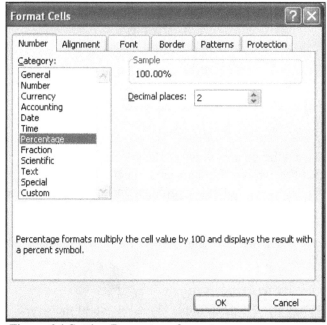

Figure 6-1 Setting Percentage format

7. **{LEFT-CLICK}** the **Number** tab.
8. **{LEFT-CLICK}** the **Percentage**.
9. Make sure the **Decimal Places** drop-down box is set to **2**.
10. **{LEFT-CLICK}** the **OK** button.

Having set the format, we need to copy the formula from cell **A10** for all of column **A**.

1. **{LEFT-CLICK}** cell **A10**.
2. **{LEFT-CLICK}** the formula bar.
3. Press the **F4** key until the formula is '= O10/$O$41'.
4. Press the **ENTER** key.
5. **{LEFT-CLICK}** cell **A10**.
6. **Hold** the **CTRL** key down while pressing the **C** key.
7. **{LEFT-CLICK}** On cell **A11**.
8. **Hold** the **SHIFT** key down.
9. **{LEFT-CLICK}** On cell **A41**.
10. **Hold** the **CTRL** key down while pressing the **V** key.
11. **{LEFT-CLICK}** cell **A10**.
12. Press the **ENTER** key

Column **A** may look similar to Figure 6-2.

		DQ
100.00%	Database Flaws	10
#DIV/0!	Screen Errors	
#DIV/0!	Report Errors	
#DIV/0!	Scope Shortages	
#DIV/0!	Program Logic Errors	
#DIV/0!	Redesign	
#DIV/0!	Scope Change	
#DIV/0!	Missing Objects	
#DIV/0!	Level Checks	
#DIV/0!	Extraneous Objects	
#DIV/0!	Gold Plating	
#DIV/0!	Pre-existing Conditions	
#DIV/0!	Critical Errors	
#DIV/0!	Installation Errors	
#DIV/0!	Training Issues	
#DIV/0!	Environmental Issues	
#DIV/0!	Cosmetic Changes	
#DIV/0!	Data Errors	
#DIV/0!	Implementation/Setup	
#DIV/0!	User Error	
#DIV/0!	Application Errors	
#DIV/0!	Typographical Errors	
#DIV/0!	I/O Omissions	
#DIV/0!		
#DIV/0!		
#DIV/0!		
#DIV/0!		
#DIV/0!		
#DIV/0!		
#DIV/0!		
#DIV/0!	Totals:	10

Figure 6-2 Divide by Zero error

This illustrates a case of a common Excel error; the **divide by zero** error. Quite simply, it occurs anytime a formula tries to divide a number by zero. It is so common that many users just ignore it.

However, it is distracting and propagates an unprofessional presentation. Besides, if the Excel developer cannot capture this basic error, one might question their abilities with other aspects of Excel.

It is actually quite easy to 'handle' this error.

1. **{LEFT-CLICK}** cell **A10**.

2. **{LEFT-CLICK} <u>Format</u>** on the top menu bar to display the formatting menu similar to Figure 6-3.

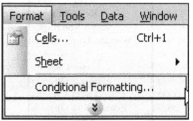

Figure 6-3 Format Menu

3. **{LEFT-CLICK} <u>Conditional Formatting</u>** to display the dialogue box shown in Figure 6-4.

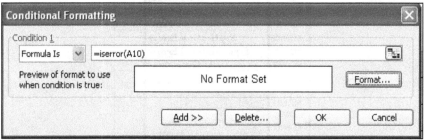

Figure 6-4 Conditional Formatting

4. **{LEFT-CLICK}** the **down-arrow** on the box under **<u>Condition 1</u>**.
5. **{LEFT-CLICK} <u>Formula is</u>**.
6. **{LEFT-CLICK}** the box to the right of the box saying **<u>Formula is</u>**.
7. Type '**=iserror(<u>A10</u>)**' (without the quotes).
8. **{LEFT-CLICK}** the **<u>Format</u>** button to display screen 6-5.

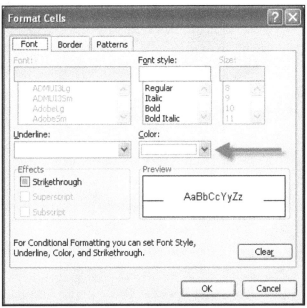

Figure 6-5 Font selection

9. **{LEFT-CLICK}** the **Color** drop down box and select the color that matches the cell color (in this case, **white**.)
10. **{LEFT-CLICK}** the **OK** button.
11. **{LEFT-CLICK}** the **OK** button again.

[For Excel 2007,
A.   *{LEFT-CLICK} cell **A10**.*
B.   *{LEFT-CLICK} **Conditional Formatting** down-arrow on the **Home** tab.*
C.   *{LEFT-CLICK} **New Rule**.*
D.   *{LEFT-CLICK} **Use a formula to determine which cells to format**.*
E.   *{LEFT-CLICK} the **format values where this formula is true:** box*
F.   Type '**=iserror(A10)**' (without the quotes).
G.   *{LEFT-CLICK} the **Format** button.*
H.   *{LEFT-CLICK} the **FONT** tab.*
I.   *{LEFT-CLICK} the **Color** down -arrow button.*
J.   *LEFT-CLICK} the **White** box (upper left).*
K.   *{LEFT-CLICK} the **OK** button].*
L.   *{LEFT-CLICK} the **OK** button].*

1. **{LEFT-CLICK}** cell **A10**.
2. **Hold** the **CTRL** key down while pressing the **C** key.
3. **{LEFT-CLICK}** On cell **A11**.
4. **Hold** the **SHIFT** key down.
5. **{LEFT-CLICK}** On cell **A41.**

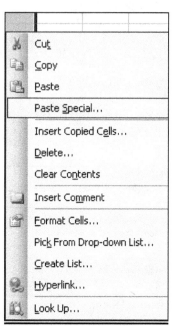

Figure 6-6 Paste Special

6. **{LEFT-CLICK}** the **EDIT** menu option to display the menu similar to Figure 6-6.

7. **{LEFT-CLICK}** On **Paste Special** to display Figure 6-7.

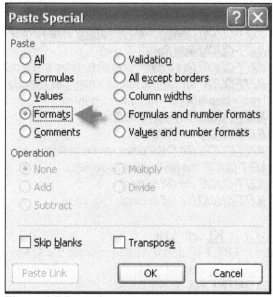

Figure 6-7 Paste formats

8. {LEFT-CLICK} On **Formats**.
9. {LEFT-CLICK} the **OK** button.

[For Excel 2007,
     A. {RIGHT-CLICK} the selected area to display the Pop-up menu.
     B. {LEFT-CLICK} PasTE Special...
     C. {LEFT-CLICK} Formats.
     D. {LEFT-CLICK} the OK button.
     E. Press the ESC key.

Now, the <u>divide by zero</u> error is masked; making for a much cleaner presentation. The error is still there, it just is not readily visible.

The other concern you might have is that the '**10**' we entered into cell **C10** may not appear to show up on the chart (depending upon your version of Excel.). Keep in mind that this is the first data element we have entered.

Since there are twelve data points we are tracking: '**DQ**' through the fourth '**HD**' and we are measuring totals, the chart may not react until an entry is made into a second data column.

As an example, {**LEFT-CLICK**} cell **D11** and type'**27**' into it, then press the **ENTER** key. Note that the chart did react to that entry. Typically, Area graphs require at least two data points (in this case, cells **C10** and **D11**).

Save your work then feel free to enter data in the data cells (**C10** through **N40**) and observe how the graph responds.

To reset, or clear, the data cells; do the following.

1. {**LEFT-CLICK**} cell **A10**.
2. **Hold** the **SHIFT** key down.
3. {**LEFT-CLICK**} On cell **N40**.
4. {**RIGHT-CLICK**} the selected area to display the pop-up menu shown in Figure 6-8.

Figure 6-8 Clear Contents

5. **{LEFT-CLICK} Clear Contents**.

The contents of the data grid are now cleared and the graph is clean. **{LEFT-CLICK}** anywhere in the selected area to 'unselect' the data grid.

Save your work.

Chapter 7

Final Thoughts

The next topic we will cover is called linkages, or links. With links, data on one page automatically updates cells on other pages that are 'linked' together. This capability is extremely powerful and relatively simple to implement. (Note: You can also 'link' spreadsheets (workbooks) together.)

For our sample exercise, we will enter some data on the **Cover** tab, then link the **Quality** tab to those data elements and then display some calculated results from the **Quality** tab on the **Cover** tab. (Sounds complicated, but it is not.)

{LEFT-CLICK} the **Cover** tab at the bottom of the screen. This will move us to the **Cover** page, which is now our active worksheet.

{LEFT-CLICK} in cell **A3** and type the following (without the quotes) pressing the **ENTER** key after each item. (You may need to change the cursor direction setting.)

> "Title:"
> "Date:"
> "Version:"
> "Development % :"
> "QA % :"
> "Help Desk % :"

Next,

1. **{LEFT-CLICK}** cell **A3**.
2. **Hold** the **SHIFT** key down.
3. **{LEFT-CLICK}** cell **A8**.
4. **{LEFT-CLICK}** the **Bold** button at the top of the screen.
5. **{LEFT-CLICK}** the **Right-justify** button at the top of the screen.

For the three percentage fields (which we will calculate with data on the **Quality** tab), we need to set the format. To do this:

1. **{LEFT-CLICK}** in cell **B6**
2. **Hold** the **SHIFT** key down.
3. **{LEFT-CLICK}** in cell **B8.**

4. **{RIGHT-CLICK}** the selected area to display the pop-up menu shown in Figure 7-1

Figure 7-1 Format Cells

5. **{LEFT-CLICK}** on **Format Cells...** to display the dialogue screen as shown in Figure 7-2.

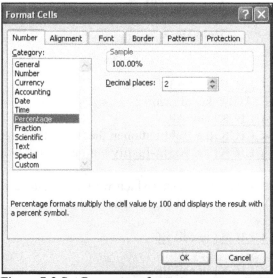

Figure 7-2 Set Percentage format

6. {LEFT-CLICK} on the **Number** tab.
7. {LEFT-CLICK} on **Percentage.**
8. Verify that the **Decimal places** are set to **2**.
9. {LEFT-CLICK} on the **Patterns** tab.

[This will be the Fill tab in Excel 2007.]

10. {LEFT-CLICK} the lightest color **yellow** on the color palette.
11. {LEFT-CLICK} the **OK** button.
12. {LEFT-CLICK} on **Format Cells...** to display the dialogue screen as shown in Figure 7-2.

13. {LEFT-CLICK} in cell **B3.**
14. **Hold** the **SHIFT** key down.
15. {LEFT-CLICK} in cell **B5.**
16. {RIGHT-CLICK} the selected area to display the pop-up menu shown in Figure 7-1.
17. {LEFT-CLICK} on **Format Cells...** to display the dialogue screen as shown in Figure 7-2.
18. {LEFT-CLICK} on the **Patterns** tab.
19. {LEFT-CLICK} the lightest color **green** on the color palette.
20. {LEFT-CLICK} the **OK** button.

Note: The color scheme is a technique I use to visually indicate the linkages:

Green cells represent static data that will be used (linked) elsewhere.
Yellow cells represent dynamic data resulting from linkages.

We need to provide some data to link to the **Quality** tab.

1. {LEFT-CLICK} cell **B3.**
2. Type: **Your Name** ' **– Quality Score Card**' (without the quotes)
3. {LEFT-CLICK} cell **B4.**
4. {LEFT-CLICK} the **Formula bar** at the top of the screen.
5. Type '**=Today()**' (without the quotes)
6. {LEFT-CLICK} cell **B5.**
7. Type: '**Version 1.01**' (without the quotes).
8. Press the **ENTER** key.

	A	B	C	D
1				
2				
3	Title:	Ron Goulden - Quality Scorecard		
4	Date:	3/30/2010		
5	Version:	Version 1.01		
6	Development %:			
7	QA %:			
8	Help Desk %:			

Figure 7-3 Cover entries

1. {DOUBLE-CLICK} the line separating columns **B** and **C** to adjust for the length of the longest element.
2. {LEFT-CLICK} cell **B3**.
3. Hold the **SHIFT** key down.
4. {LEFT-CLICK} cell **B5**.
5. {LEFT-CLICK} the **Left-justify** button.

At this point, the **Cover** tab should look similar to Figure 7-3.

Note: if the date is incorrect;

1. {RIGHT-CLICK} cell **B4** to display the pop-up menu shown in Figure 7-1
2. {LEFT-CLICK} **Format Cells…**.
3. {LEFT-CLICK} on the **Number** tab.
4. {LEFT-CLICK} on **Date**.
5. {LEFT-CLICK} on the **type** that matches the format in Figure 7-3. (For the example in Figure 7-3, it would be '***3/14/2001**'. (Figure 7-4)
6. {LEFT-CLICK} the **OK** button.

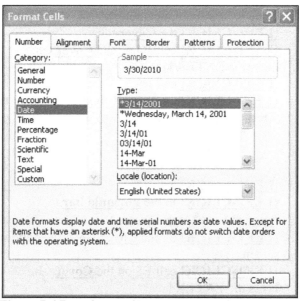
Figure 7-4 Date formatting

Save your work.

Now, we will begin linking our spreadsheets together.

1. **{LEFT-CLICK}** on the **Quality** tab at the bottom of the screen to switch to the **Quality** spreadsheet.
2. **{LEFT-CLICK}** cell **B4** (the **Formula bar** should say "**Quality Scorecard**')
3. **{LEFT-CLICK}** in the **Formula bar** and delete '**Quality Scorecard**'
4. type '=' (without the quotes.)
5. **{LEFT-CLICK}** on the **Cover** tab at the bottom of the screen
6. **{LEFT-CLICK}** cell **B3** in the **Cover** tab
7. Press the **ENTER** key.

The screen should have shifted back to the **Quality** tab and the title should now say '**<Your Name> - Quality Scorecard**'. If you return to the **Cover** tab and change the title, the change will be reflected on the **Quality** tab.

1. **{LEFT-CLICK}** on the **Quality** tab at the bottom of the screen
2. **{LEFT-CLICK}** cell **B6**
3. **{LEFT-CLICK}** in the **Formula bar.**

4. **Type '='** (without the quotes).
5. **{LEFT-CLICK}** the **Cover** tab.
6. **{LEFT-CLICK}** cell **B4** on the **Cover** tab.
7. Press the **ENTER** key.
8. **{LEFT-CLICK}** cell **B6**.
9. **{LEFT-CLICK}** on the **Left-Justify** button at the top of the screen.

Next,

1. **{LEFT-CLICK}** cell **B7**.
2. **{LEFT-CLICK}** in the **Formula bar**.
3. **type '='** (without the quotes.)
4. **{LEFT-CLICK}** on the **Cover** tab at the bottom of the screen.
5. **{LEFT-CLICK}** cell **B5** on the **Cover** tab.
6. Press the **ENTER** key.
7. **{LEFT-CLICK}** cell **B7**.
8. **{LEFT-CLICK}** the **Left-Justify** button at the top of the screen

At this point, we are linking to static (constant) data that exists on the **Cover** tab. Our next exercise will be to go to the **Cover** tab and link to dynamic (changing) data from the **Quality** tab.

Save your work.

1. **{LEFT-CLICK}** on the **Cover** tab at the bottom of the screen (You may need to **{DOUBLE-CLICK}** the line between column **A** and column **B** to adjust the size of column **A**.)
2. **{LEFT-CLICK}** cell **B6** in the **Cover** tab.
3. **{LEFT-CLICK}** in the **Formula bar**.
4. **Type '='** (without the quotes.)
5. **{LEFT-CLICK}** on the **Quality** tab at the bottom of the screen.
6. **{LEFT-CLICK}** cell **F42**.
7. **Type '/'** (without the quotes.)
8. **{LEFT-CLICK}** cell **O41**.
9. Press the **ENTER** key.

(Do not worry about the <u>divide by zero error</u>... we'll correct that momentarily).

110

1. **{LEFT-CLICK}** cell **B7** on the **Cover** tab.
2. **{LEFT-CLICK}** in the **Formula bar.**
3. **Type '='** (without the quotes.)
4. **{LEFT-CLICK}** on the **Quality** tab at the bottom of the screen.
5. **{LEFT-CLICK}** cell **J42**.
6. **Type '/'** (without the quotes.)
7. **{LEFT-CLICK}** cell **O41**.
8. Press the **ENTER** key.

1. **{LEFT-CLICK}** cell **B8** in the **Cover** tab.
2. **{LEFT-CLICK}** in the **Formula bar.**
3. **Type '='** (without the quotes.)
4. **{LEFT-CLICK}** on the **Quality** tab at the bottom of the screen.
5. **{LEFT-CLICK}** cell **N42**.
6. **Type '/'** (without the quotes.)
7. **{LEFT-CLICK}** cell **O41**.
8. Press the **ENTER** key.

Now, we need to correct the divide by zero error in cells **B6** through **B8** on the **Cover** tab.

1. **{LEFT-CLICK}** cell **B6**.
2. **{LEFT-CLICK} Format** on the top menu bar to display the formatting menu similar to Figure 7-5.

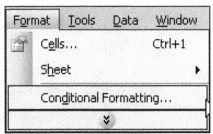

Figure 7-5 Format menu

3. **{LEFT-CLICK} Conditional Formatting** to display the dialogue box shown in Figure 7-6.

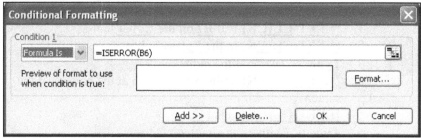

Figure 7-6 Conditional Formatting

4. **{LEFT-CLICK}** the **down-arrow** on the box under **Condition 1**.
5. **{LEFT-CLICK} Formula is**.
6. **{LEFT-CLICK}** in the box to the right of the box saying **Formula is**.
7. Type '**=iserror(B6)**' (without the quotes).
8. **{LEFT-CLICK}** the **Format** button to display screen 7-7.

[For Excel 2007,

A. *{LEFT-CLICK} Conditional Formatting down-arrow on the Home tab.*
B. *{LEFT-CLICK} New Rule.*
C. *{LEFT-CLICK} Use a formula to determine which cells to format.*
D. *{LEFT-CLICK} the format values where this formula is true: box.*
E. Type '**=iserror(B6)**' (without the quotes).
F. *{LEFT-CLICK} the Format button.*
G. *{LEFT-CLICK} the Color drop-down button.*
H. *{LEFT-CLICK} the shade of yellow that matches the Fill.*
I. *{LEFT-CLICK} the OK button].*
J. *{LEFT-CLICK} the OK button].*

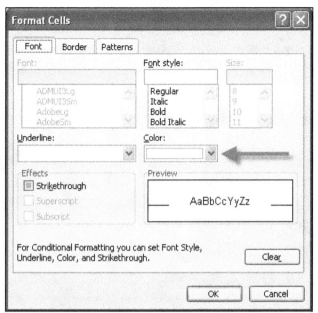
Figure 7-7 Font selection

9. **{LEFT-CLICK}** the **Color** drop down box and select the color that matches the cell color (in this case, **Light Yellow** as shown in Figure 7-8)

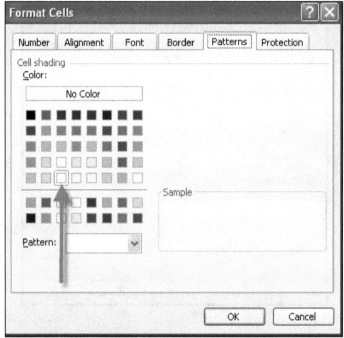

Figure 7-8 - Light Yellow selection

10. **{LEFT-CLICK}** the **OK** button.
11. **{LEFT-CLICK}** the **OK** button again.
12. **{LEFT-CLICK}** cell **B6**.
13. **Hold** the **CTRL** key down while pressing the **C** key.
14. **{LEFT-CLICK}** cell **B7**.
15. **Hold** the **SHIFT** key down.
16. **{LEFT-CLICK}** cell **B8.**

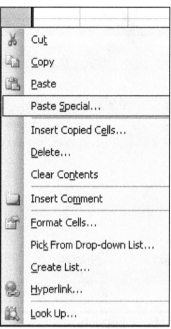

Figure 7-9 Paste Special

17. **{LEFT-CLICK}** the **Edit** menu option to display the menu similar to Figure 7-10.

[For Excel 2007, {RIGHT-CLICK} the selected area.]

18. **{LEFT-CLICK}** On **Paste Special** to display Figure 7-9.

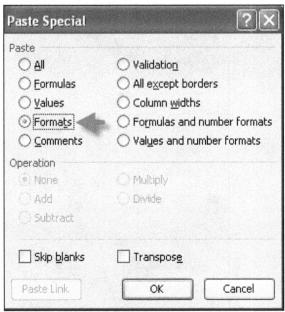

Figure 7-10 Paste Formats

19. **{LEFT-CLICK} Formats**.

Note that we use the **FORMAT** selection rather than the **FORMULAS** selection (even though we used a formula to determine the formatting).

20. **{LEFT-CLICK}** the **OK** button.
21. Press the **ESC** key or **{LEFT-CLICK}** close outside of the selection area to close the copy selection.

Now, the **divide by zero** error is masked; making for a much cleaner presentation. Remember that the error is still there, it just is not readily visible.

For a bit of clean-up:
1. **{LEFT-CLICK}** cell **B6**.
2. **Hold** the **SHIFT** key down.
3. **{LEFT-CLICK}** cell **B8**.
4. **{LEFT-CLICK}** the **Left-Justify** button.
5. Press the **ESC** key.

Since we only masked the error, we need to provide a few more formulae on the **Quality** tab to make our linkages work correctly and actually display data.

1. **{LEFT-CLICK}** on the **Quality** tab at the bottom of the screen.
2. **{LEFT-CLICK}** cell **F42** in the **Quality** tab.
3. **{LEFT-CLICK}** the **Autosum** button The **Autosum** button has the uppercase sigma character ($\sum$) on it. (Figure 7-11).

*[For Excel 2007, it is on the **Formulas** tab.]*

Figure 7-11 Autosum button

4. **{LEFT-CLICK}** cell **C41**.
5. **Hold** the **SHIFT** key down.
6. **{LEFT-CLICK}** cell **F41**.
7. **Press** the **ENTER** key.

8. **{LEFT-CLICK}** cell **F42**.
9. **Hold** the **CTRL** key down while pressing the **C** key.
10. **{LEFT-CLICK}** cell **J42**.
11. **Hold** the **CTRL** key down.
12. **{LEFT-CLICK}** cell **N42**.
13. **Hold** the **CTRL** key down and press the **V** key.
14. Press the **ESC** key to close the copy selection.

Now we are ready to test the dynamic links between the **Quality** and **Cover** tabs.

Randomly type numbers in the data range of cells **C10** through **N40**. Note that the totals will update on the **Quality** tab. Occasionally move to the **Cover** tab and note that the percentages update as the data on the **Quality** tab changes.

Save your work.

Next, we will perform a few 'clean-up' functions to ensure a more presentable document.

1. **{LEFT-CLICK}** on the **Quality** tab at the bottom of the screen.

2. Type some values in the cell range **C10** to **N40**.
3. **{LEFT-CLICK}** cell **C10** on the **Quality** tab.
4. **Hold** the **SHIFT** key down.
5. **{LEFT-CLICK}** cell **N42**.
6. **LEFT-CLICK}** the **BOLD** tool (the letter 'B') as shown in Figure 7-12.
7. If the values in the cell range **C10** to **N42** become un-bolded, **LEFT-CLICK}** the **BOLD** tool (the letter 'B') again.

Figure 7-12 Bold tool button

8. **{LEFT-CLICK}** the **Center** button, as shown in Figure 7-13.
9. If the values in the cell range **C10** to **N42** become un-centered, **LEFT-CLICK}** the **Center** button again.
10. Press the **ESC** key.

Figure7-13 Center tool button

Now, the data range and the totals are bolded and centered in the cells, providing a standard presentation.

Our next step is to provide the ability to document some of the conditions we have entered in the data range. To do this, we will add a new 'page' to the **Quality** tab.

1. **{LEFT-CLICK}** on the **Quality** tab at the bottom of the screen.
2. **{LEFT-CLICK}** cell **A45** on the **Quality** tab.
3. **{LEFT-CLICK}** the **Insert** menu item at the top of the screen

118

*[For Excel 2007, it is on the **Page Layout** tab.]*

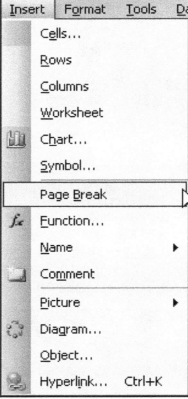

Figure 7-14 Add <u>Page Break</u>

4. {LEFT-CLICK} Page Break.

[For Excel 2007,
*A. {LEFT-CLICK} the **Breaks** down-arrow.*
*B. {LEFT-CLICK} **Insert Page Break**.]*

Note that a dashed line appears between rows 44 and 45.

(It may not be visible for Excel 2007.)

5. {LEFT-CLICK} cell B46.
6. **Hold** the **SHIFT** key down.
7. {LEFT-CLICK} cell AC55.
8. {LEFT-CLICK} the **Borders** button **down-arrow** (shown in Figure 7-15)

119

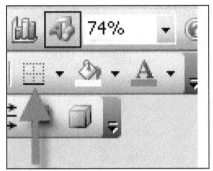
Figure 7-15 Border button

9. From the pop-up menu, **{LEFT-CLICK}** the **Thick Outline** button,
10. **{LEFT-CLICK}** cell **B46**.
11. Type '**Defects**' (without the quotes).
12. **Press** the **ENTER** key.
13. **{LEFT-CLICK}** cell **B46**.
14. **{LEFT-CLICK}** the **Bold** button (Figure 7-16).
15. **{LEFT-CLICK}** the **Center** button.

Figure 7-16 **Bold** and **Merge** (**Center**) buttons

16. **{LEFT-CLICK}** cell **C46**.
17. **Hold** the **SHIFT** key down.
18. **{LEFT-CLICK}** cell **AC46**.
19. **{LEFT-CLICK}** the **Borders** button
20. From the pop-up menu, **{LEFT-CLICK}** the **Outline** button.
21. **{LEFT-CLICK}** the **Merge** button (Figure 7-17).

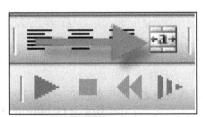
Figure 7-17 **Merge** button

22. Type '**Description**' (without the quotes).
23. Press the ENTER key.
24. **{LEFT-CLICK} cell C46.**
25. {LEFT-CLICK} the **Bold** button (Figure 7-16).
26. If necessary, **{LEFT-CLICK}** the **Center** button.

Now, we are ready to add a little automation to the documentation 'page' of the **Quality** tab.

1. **{LEFT-CLICK} cell A47.**
2. Type '**1**' (without the quotes).
3. Press the ENTER key (the cursor should have moved down to cell **A48**).
4. Type =**IF(B47 <>"",A47+1,"")** and press the ENTER key. (Note: this uses pairs of **double quotes** rather than four single quotes).
5. {LEFT-CLICK} cell **A48**.
6. **Hold** the CTRL key down and press the **C** key.
7. {LEFT-CLICK} cell **A49**.
8. **Hold** the SHIFT key down.
9. {LEFT-CLICK} cell **A55**.
10. **Hold** the CTRL key down and press the **V** key.
11. {LEFT-CLICK} cell **A47**.
12. **Hold** the SHIFT key down.
13. {LEFT-CLICK} cell **A55**.
14. {LEFT-CLICK} the **Bold** button (Figure 7-16).
15. {LEFT-CLICK} the **Center** button.
16. **Press** the ESC key.

At first glance, this exercise appears to have accomplished little. However, **{LEFT-CLICK}** cell **B47** and type "**Issue #1   (12/12/06 13:47)**" (without the quotes) and press the ENTER key. Note that the value of cell **A48** automatically incremented to '**2**'.

Be aware that if rows are inserted, the formula must be 're-pasted' to ensure proper numbering.

Note that by using CTRL-V to paste the **formula** rather than the **Paste Special...** some of the borders may have 'disappeared'.

1. **{LEFT-CLICK} cell A46.**
2. **Hold** the SHIFT key down.

3. {LEFT-CLICK} cell **A55**.
4. {LEFT-CLICK} the **Borders down-arrow** button
5. From the pop-up menu, {LEFT-CLICK} the **Outline** button.

There are just a few more 'touches' to add to our work.

1. **LEFT-CLICK}** the line separating columns **B** and **C**.
2. **While** holding the left mouse button down, drag the cursor to the right until the text fits completely in cell **B47**.)
3. **{LEFT-CLICK}** cell **B47**.
4. **Hold** the **SHIFT** key down.
5. **{LEFT-CLICK}** cell **B55**.
6. **{RIGHT-CLICK}** the selected area to display the formatting pop-up menu.
7. **{LEFT-CLICK}** the **Format Cells...** option.
8. **{LEFT-CLICK}** the **Border** tab.

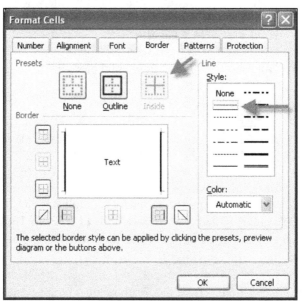

Figure 7-18 Dotted Line selection

9. **{LEFT-CLICK}** the '**Dotted Line**' style.
10. **{LEFT-CLICK}** the **Inside** button.
11. **{LEFT-CLICK}** the lightest solid line style.
12. **{LEFT-CLICK}** the '**Right**' vertical border.
13. **{LEFT-CLICK}** the '**Top**' Horizontal border.
14. **{LEFT-CLICK}** the **OK** button.

122

We will perform a similar operation for the Description area, but instead of using the **Inside** preset, we will select the interior line.

15. **{LEFT-CLICK}** cell **C47**.
16. **Hold** the **SHIFT** key down.
17. **{LEFT-CLICK}** cell **AC55**.
18. **{RIGHT-CLICK}** the selected area to display the formatting pop-up menu.
19. **{LEFT-CLICK}** the **Format Cells...** option.
20. **{LEFT-CLICK}** the **Border** tab.

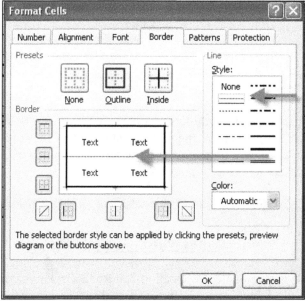

Figure 7-19 Dotted Interior lines

21. **{LEFT-CLICK}** the '**Dotted Line**' style.
22. **{LEFT-CLICK}** the **Center** Horizontal line as shown in Figure 7-19.
23. **{LEFT-CLICK}** the **OK** button.

We need to make our description area easier to work with. To accomplish this, we will select and merge cells.

1. **{LEFT-CLICK}** cell **C47**.
2. **Hold** the **SHIFT** key down.
3. **{LEFT-CLICK}** cell **AC47**.

123

4. {LEFT-CLICK} the **Merge** button.
5. Repeat this process for rows **48** through **55**.
6. {LEFT-CLICK} cell **C47**.
7. **Hold** the **SHIFT** key down.
8. {LEFT-CLICK} cell **C55**.
9. {LEFT-CLICK} the **Left-Justify** button.
10. {LEFT-CLICK} cell **C47**.
11. Type "**Module V193 requires three additional database fields to accomplish X-Y-Z camera coordinates.**" (Without the quotes.)
12. Press the **ENTER** key.

45				
46		**Defects**		**Description**
47	1	Issue #1 (12/12/06 13:47)	Module V193 requires three additional database fields to accommodate X-Y-Z camera coordinates.	
48	2			
49				
50				
51				
52				
53				
54				
55				

Figure 7-20 Documentation page

The documentation page should look similar to Figure 7-20. If additional lines are added, simply use the **Insert** menu at the top of the screen and select **Rows**. (Again, any time rows are inserted, the formula in column **A** must be 're-pasted' to ensure proper numbering.)

[For Excel 2007, {RIGHT-CLICK} the Row number and {LEFT-CLICK} Insert]

Save your work.

Multi-line text is a valuable presentation feature that again is quite simple to implement with Excel, though many casual users are unaware of the mechanics.

For this exercise, we will combine adjacent cells in a column and type some simple multi-line text, just to illustrate the feature.

1. **{LEFT-CLICK}** cell **B60**.
2. **Hold** the **SHIFT** key down.
3. **{LEFT-CLICK}** cell **B65**.
4. **{LEFT-CLICK}** the **Merge** button (Figure 7-17).

The result of this action is that we have a cell that spans six rows.

1. **{LEFT-CLICK}** cell **B60**.

2. **{LEFT-CLICK}** the **Formula bar**.
3. Type '**The steps are:** '(without the quotes).
4. Press the **ENTER** key.
5. **{LEFT-CLICK }** the selected area (**B60**).
6. **{RIGHT-CLICK}** the selected area to display the formatting pop-up menu.
7. **{LEFT-CLICK}** **Format Cells…**
8. **{LEFT-CLICK}** the **Alignment** tab (See Figure 7-21).

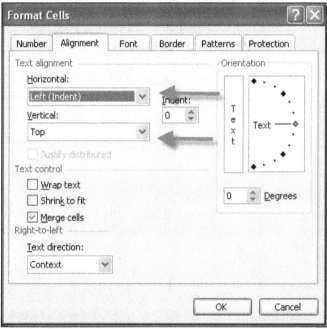

Figure 7-21Top Alignment

2. Change the **Horizontal** Alignment to '**Left (indent)**'.
3. Change the **Vertical** Alignment to '**Top**'.
4. **{LEFT-CLICK }** the **OK** button.

Looking at Figure 7-21, note that the **Merge Cells** box is checked. This is a result of our previous operation. This indicates that you can select a range of cells, go to the format dialogue box and merge them with a click of the mouse. Note the **Wrap Text** box.

1. **{LEFT-CLICK}** cell **B60.**

The **Formula bar** at the top of the screen should say. "**The Steps Are:**"

2. **{LEFT-CLICK}** the **Formula bar** to the right of "**The Steps are:**'.

125

3. Type "**1 – Initiate 2 – Plan 3 – Execute 4 – Monitor 5 – Close-out**".
4. Press the **ENTER** key

Note that some of the text appears to be 'chopped off' in our merged cells.

This can be partially addressed with the **Wrap Text** box in Figure 7-21.

1. **{LEFT-CLICK}** cell **B60**.
2. **{RIGHT-CLICK}** the selected area to display the formatting pop-up menu.
3. **{LEFT-CLICK} Format Cells...**
4. **{LEFT-CLICK}** the **Alignment** tab.
5. **{LEFT-CLICK}** the **Wrap Text** checkbox (See Figure 7-20).
6. **{LEFT-CLICK }** the **OK** button.

While this shows the entire string of text, it still appears unformatted. To correct this:

1. **{LEFT-CLICK}** cell **B60**.
2. **{LEFT-CLICK}** the **Formula bar** to the left of "**1 – Initiate**".
3. Hold the **ALT** key down and press the **ENTER** key. (Note that the **Formula bar** may have expanded downward and the second line begins with "**1 – Initiate**").
4. Press the **SPACE** bar five times.
5. **Repeat** the process for each numbered item in the list.
6. Press the **ENTER** key after all five items in the list have been adjusted.

The steps are:
1 – Initiate
2 – Plan
3 – Execute
4 – Monitor
5 – Close-out

Figure 7-22 Results of <u>ALT-ENTER</u>

Looking at Figure 7-22, we now have 'formatted' text in a merged cell. The point to remember is to use **ALT-ENTER** combination in the **Formula bar** to create a new line, and press the **ENTER** key only after the formatting is finished.

 Remember that checking the **Wrap Text** box will force the text to remain within the borders of the cell, 'wrapping' the text to successive lines. As an experiment,

1. **{LEFT-CLICK}** cell **C57**.
2. **{LEFT-CLICK}** the **Formula bar**.
3. Type '=' (Without the quotes).
4. **{LEFT-CLICK}** cell **C47**.
5. Press the **ENTER** key.
6. **{RIGHT-CLICK}** the selected area to display the formatting pop-up menu.
7. **{LEFT-CLICK} Format Cells...**
8. **{LEFT-CLICK}** the **Alignment** tab (See Figure 7-21).
9. **{LEFT-CLICK}** the **Wrap Text** box.
10. **{LEFT-CLICK }** the **OK** button.
11. **{LEFT-CLICK}** cell **C57**.
12. If necessary, **{DOUBLE-CLICK}** the line between rows **56** and **57**.

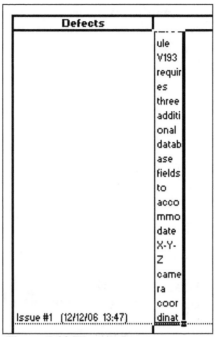

Defects	
	ule
	V193
	requir
	es
	three
	additi
	onal
	datab
	ase
	fields
	to
	acco
	mmo
	date
	X-Y-
	Z
	came
	ra
	coor
Issue #1 (12/12/06 13:47)	dinat

Figure 7-23 Wrapped text

Looking at Figure 7-23, you can see that the text has been 'adjusted' to fit within the width of the column.

To reverse this, either **{LEFT-CLICK }** the **Edit** menu option at the top of the screen and **{LEFT-CLICK }** the **Undo Format Cells** (Or repeat steps 1 through 6 above).

*[For Excel 2007, {LEFT-CLICK} the **Clear** Icon on the **Home** tab.*

In closing, you should now have a comfortable grasp of Excel and its capabilities. You also have a fully functioning, linked Quality Score Card. While the Score Card we developed is aimed at specific Programming and Project Management areas, it can easily be adapted to other professions.

By simply modifying the **Cover** tab and changing the contents of rows **8** and **9** and column **B** on the **Quality** tab, the score card can report virtually anything that can be measured.

If you want multiple score cards in a single workbook,

1. **{LEFT-CLICK }** the **Edit** menu option at the top of the screen.
2. **{LEFT-CLICK }** the **down-arrows** to expand the menu.

3. {LEFT-CLICK} MOVE OR COPY SPREADSHEET.
4. **{LEFT-CLICK}** (MOVE TO END).
5. **{LEFT-CLICK}** the CREATE A COPY checkbox.
6. {LEFT-CLICK} the **OK** button.

[For Excel 2007,
1. **{LEFT-CLICK}** the **HOME** 'tab.
2. **{LEFT-CLICK}** the **FORMAT** icon **down-arrow**.
3. **{LEFT-CLICK}** **MOVE OR COPY SHEET...**
4. **{LEFT-CLICK}** **(MOVE TO END).**
5. **{LEFT-CLICK}** the **CREATE A COPY** checkbox.
6. **{LEFT-CLICK}** the **OK** button.]

A new spreadsheet tab will appear called **QUALITY (2)**. Simply rename the tab and adjust the linkages as necessary.

This can include budgets, homework assignments, employee performance. The adaptability is unlimited.

Save your work.

Inserting a Picture

[The following exercises will reference Excel 2007, but at this point it should be a simple transition to earlier versions of Excel. The commands and functions are the same; they may be at different locations.]

Looking at the cover of the book, our spreadsheet is missing a notable characteristic. The logo is missing. For all practical purposes, a logo is merely a picture that we will include as a part of our spreadsheet. While you can use any picture file on your computer, for the sake of consistency, we will use the '**Goulden Systems Cybernetics**' logo.

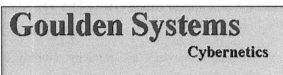

Figure 7-24 Logo

To obtain this logo file,

   A. Start a web browser of you choosing and go to
      http://www.rongoulden.com/Literary.htm

   B. At the top of the page, you will see a logo image that says **Goulden Systems Cybernetics** (Refer to figure 7-24.).

   C. {**RIGHT-CLICK**} the image to display a pop-up menu.

   D. {**LEFT-CLICK**} 'Save target As…'.

   E. In the **Save** dialogue, locate the directory you created for your spreadsheet (**C:_Goulden_Excel**).

   F. For the **file name**, type 'GSC'. (It may already default to that.)

   G. The **Save as Type** should be **JPG** file. (Again, it may already default to that.)

   H. {**LEFT-CLICK**} the **SAVE** button.

   I. If you get a message that the file already exists, left-click the **Yes** button. (Since you are in a dedicated directory, it is doubtful that you already have an image file there.)

Return to your spreadsheet.

   A. {**LEFT-CLICK**} cell **P1.**

B. {**LEFT-CLICK**} the **Insert** menu option.

C. {**LEFT-CLICK**} **Picture**.

D. {**LEFT-CLICK**} **Insert Picture from file.**

E. Navigate to the **C:_Goulden_Excel** directory.

F. {**LEFT-CLICK**} the file named **GSC.**

G. {**LEFT-CLICK**} the **INSERT** button.

The logo should appear at the top of the spreadsheet.

A. {**LEFT-CLICK**} the image to display the handles (small boxes or circles used to adjust the size of the image.

B. {**LEFT-CLICK**} the lower right corner of the image.

C. **Hold** the **left** mouse button **down** while moving the mouse **down** and to the **right** until the right side of the image is at the right edge of column **S**.

If the image is not centered to your liking,

A. {**LEFT-CLICK**} the image (not the handles).

B. **Hold** the **left** mouse button **down** and drag the image where you want it. You may want to fine-tune the size adjustment as well.

While we used a logo for this example, remember that any picture file may be added and adjusted to meet your needs.

Inserting a 'Smart' Symbol

Sometimes, it may be beneficial to provide a visual clue about the quality of the data being presented. Some people use 'traffic lights', 'stop signs', 'happy/sad faces' 'thumbs up/down' symbols, etc.

The next exercise is a 'bonus' that may prove entertaining and educational. The steps listed below will be for Excel 2007, though you should have little difficulty converting to earlier versions of Excel.

131

What I call a 'Smart' symbol is merely a common symbol with a slight amount of intelligence added to it to automate the presentation.

We will use the **Happy** and **Sad** faces for our demonstration.

To set up the **Happy Face** indicator,

A. **{LEFT-CLICK}** cell **W1.**
B. Hold the CTRL key **down** and **{LEFT-CLICK}** cell **X1.**
C. Hold the CTRL key **down** and **{LEFT-CLICK}** cell **A4.**
D. **{RIGHT-CLICK}** the selection area to display the **Options** menu.
E. **{LEFT-CLICK} Format Cells...**
F. **{LEFT-CLICK}** the **Font** tab.
G. In the **Font** selection box, **{LEFT-CLICK}** the **slider bar** (on the right side of the selection box) and drag it to the bottom of the list.
H. **{LEFT-CLICK}** the **Wingdings** font.
I. **{LEFT-CLICK}** the **OK** button.
J. **{RIGHT-CLICK}** cell **W1.**
K. **{LEFT-CLICK}** the **Insert** menu option (at the top of the screen).
L. **{LEFT-CLICK} Symbol** (or **Insert Symbol**) A chart of symbols should display and **Wingdings** should already be the default font style. (If the font type is not **Wingdings**, drag the scroll bar **down** and **{LEFT-CLICK}** the **Wingdings** font).
M. Locate the **Happy Face** Symbol ☺. (You may need to drag the scroll bar down to locate it.)
N. **{LEFT-CLICK}** the **Happy Face** symbol.
O. **{LEFT-CLICK}** the **Insert** button.
P. **{LEFT-CLICK}** the **Close** button.

A small **Happy Face** should be visible in cell **W1.**

To set up the **Sad Face** indicator,

A. {LEFT-CLICK} cell **X1.**
B. {LEFT-CLICK} the **Insert** menu option (at the top of the screen).
C. {LEFT-CLICK} **Symbol** (or **Insert Symbol**). A chart of symbols should display and **Wingdings** should already be the default font style. . (If the font type is not **Wingdings**, drag the scroll bar down and {LEFT-CLICK} the **Wingdings** font).
D. Locate the **Sad Face** Symbol ☹. (You may need to drag the scroll bar down to locate it.)
E. {LEFT-CLICK} the **Sad Face** symbol.
F. {LEFT-CLICK} the **Insert** button.
G. {LEFT-CLICK} the **Close** button.

A small **Sad Face** should be visible in cell **X1**.

Now, we are going to make cell **A4** the 'Smart' indicator cell. If our total number of defects is greater than 99, we will display the **Sad Face** ☹. If the defects are less than 100, we will display the **Happy Face** ☺.

These numbers are arbitrary and are for demonstration purposes. In reality, your needs will determine the relative importance of your data.

To set up the indicator cell,

A. {LEFT-CLICK} cell **A4.**
B. {RIGHT-CLICK} cell **A4** to display the **Options** menu.
C. {LEFT-CLICK} **Format Cells...**
D. {LEFT-CLICK} the **Font** tab.
E. In the **Font** selection box, {LEFT-CLICK} the **slider bar** (on the right side of the selection box) and drag it to the bottom of the list.
F. {LEFT-CLICK} the **Wingdings** font.
G. {LEFT-CLICK} the **Bold** font style.
H. Change the **Font size** to **24.**
I. {LEFT-CLICK} the **OK** button.

J. {LEFT-CLICK} the **Center** button (on the **Home** tab.)

K. {LEFT-CLICK} the **Formula bar**.

L. Type '=IF($O$41<100,$W$1,IF($O$41>99,$X$1,""))' (Without the leading and trailing single quote.)

M. Press the ENTER key.

A **Happy Face** symbol should display in cell **A4**. To test our formula,

A. {LEFT-CLICK} cell.

B. Type '**101**' (without the single quotes).

C. Press the ENTER key.

D. The **Happy Face** should have changed to a **Sad Face**.

E. {LEFT-CLICK} cell **H21** .

F. Type '**99**' (without the single quotes).

G. Press the ENTER key.

H. The **Sad Face** should have changed back to a **Happy Face.**

I. Clear the contents of cell **H21**. (Note that the **Happy Face** still shows in cell **A4**.

Since we do not want the indicator to display if there is no data represented, we will correct the **Happy Face** problem by adding a bit more 'intelligence' to cell **A4**.

First, we will test for **Sad Face** conditions, where we have more than 100 defects.

A. {LEFT-CLICK} cell **A4.**

B. {LEFT-CLICK} the **Home** tab.

C. {LEFT-CLICK} the **Conditional Formatting down-arrow**.

D. {LEFT-CLICK} **New Rule…**

E. {LEFT-CLICK} **Use a formula to determine which cells to format.**

F. {LEFT-CLICK} the formula box in the **New Formatting Rule** dialogue.

G. Type '=$O$41 >99' (without the quotes).

H. {LEFT-CLICK} the **Format** button.

I. {**LEFT-CLICK**} the **Font** tab.
J. {**LEFT-CLICK**} the **Bold** font style.
K. Set the FONT SIZE to '**24'.** (This may not be available, do not worry about it now.)
L. **LEFT-CLICK**} the **Font Color down-arrow**
M. **LEFT-CLICK**} the **yellow** font color.
N. {**LEFT-CLICK**} the **Fill** tab.
O. **LEFT-CLICK**} the **Red** fill color.
P. {**LEFT-CLICK**} the **OK** button.
Q. {**LEFT-CLICK**} the **OK** button.
R. {**LEFT-CLICK**} the **OK** button.

To test this,

A. {**LEFT-CLICK**} cell **H21**.
B. Type '**101**' (without the single quotes).
C. Press the **ENTER** key.

Cell **A4** should have a **yellow Sad Face** with a red background.

A. {**LEFT-CLICK**} cell **H21**.
B. Press the **DEL** key.

Next, we will test for **Happy Face** conditions, where we have less than 100 defects.

A. {**LEFT-CLICK**} cell **A4.**
B. {**LEFT-CLICK**} the **Home** tab.
C. {**LEFT-CLICK**} the **Conditional Formatting down-arrow**.
D. {**LEFT-CLICK**} **New Rule…**
E. {**LEFT-CLICK**} **Use a formula to determine which cells to format.**
F. {**LEFT-CLICK**} the formula box in the **New Formatting Rule** dialogue.
G. Type '=$O$41 <100' (without the quotes).
H. {**LEFT-CLICK**} the **Format** button.

135

I.   {**LEFT-CLICK**} the **Font** tab.
J.   Make sure the Font is **WingDings**.
K.   {**LEFT-CLICK**} the **Bold** font style.
L.   Set the FONT SIZE to '**24**'. (If this not available, do not worry about it now.)
M.   **LEFT-CLICK**} the **Font Color down-arrow**
N.   **LEFT-CLICK**} the **black** font color.
O.   {**LEFT-CLICK**} the **Fill** tab.
P.   **LEFT-CLICK**} the **Green** fill color.
Q.   {**LEFT-CLICK**} the **OK** button.
R.   {**LEFT-CLICK**} the **OK** button.
S.   {**LEFT-CLICK**} the **OK** button.

To test this,

A.   {**LEFT-CLICK**} cell **H21**.
B.   Type '**101**' (without the single quotes).
C.   Press the ENTER key.

Cell **A4** should have a **yellow Sad Face** with a **red** background.

A.   {**LEFT-CLICK**} cell **H21**.
B.   Type '**10**' (without the single quotes).
C.   Press the ENTER key.

Cell **A4** should have a **black Happy Face** with a **green** background.

A.   {**LEFT-CLICK**} cell **H21**.
B.   Press the DEL key.
C.   Press the ENTER key.

Note that cell **A4** still has a **black Happy Face** symbol.

We need to correct this problem. When there is no data, we do not want to display any indicator. To fix this,

A. {LEFT-CLICK} cell **A4.**
B. {LEFT-CLICK} the **Home** tab.
C. {LEFT-CLICK} the **Conditional Formatting down-arrow**.
D. {LEFT-CLICK} **New Rule…**
E. {LEFT-CLICK} **Use a formula to determine which cells to format.**
F. {LEFT-CLICK} the formula box in the **New Formatting Rule** dialogue.
G. Type '=$O$41=0' (without the quotes).
H. {LEFT-CLICK} the **Format** button.
I. {LEFT-CLICK} the **Font** tab.
J. **LEFT-CLICK}** the **Font Color down-arrow.**
K. **LEFT-CLICK}** the **White** font color.
L. {LEFT-CLICK} the **Fill** tab.
M. **LEFT-CLICK}** the **White** fill color.
N. {LEFT-CLICK} the **OK** button.
O. {LEFT-CLICK} the **OK** button.
P. {LEFT-CLICK} the **OK** button.

To test this,

A. {LEFT-CLICK} cell **H21**.
B. Type '**0**' (without the single quotes).
C. Press the **ENTER** key.

Cell **A4** should be blank.

D. {LEFT-CLICK} cell **H21**.
E. Type '**99**' (without the single quotes).
F. Press the **ENTER** key.

Cell **A4** should have a **black Happy Face** with a **green** background.

G. {LEFT-CLICK} cell **H21**.
H. Type '**101**' (without the single quotes).

I. Press the **ENTER** key.

Cell **A4** still has a **yellow Sad Face** with a **red** background.

J. {**LEFT-CLICK**} cell **H21**.
K. Press the **DEL** key.
L. Press the **ENTER** key.

Cell **A4** should be blank.

There is one final bit of house-keeping to do. We need to conceal the happy and sad faces in cells **W1** and **X1**.

A. {**LEFT-CLICK**} cell **W1**.
B. Hold the **CTRL** key **down**.
C. {**LEFT-CLICK**} cell **X1**.
D. {**RIGHT-CLICK**} the selection area to display the **Options** menu.
E. {**LEFT-CLICK**} **Format Cells…**
F. {**LEFT-CLICK**} the **Font** tab.
G. {**LEFT-CLICK**} the **Color down-arrow**.
H. {**LEFT-CLICK**} the **White** font color.
I. {**LEFT-CLICK**} the **OK** button.

The two symbols are now concealed. Note that we made extensive use of absolute addressing in this exercise.

Save your work.

At this point, you should have a good grasp of the basic Excel capabilities and should be able to navigate through spreadsheets with little difficulty.

Chapter 8

Quality by Design

There are countless philosophies regarding Quality Assurance and how to achieve 'Zero Defects' in a manufacturing or production environment. Less effort has been expended in defining the quality requirements for a software development environment. Standards such as ISO9000 and ISO14725 have been developed for the more traditional environments and industries. However Corporate Information Services Departments lag behind.

Borrowing heavily from one of the most regulated industries in the world, American Food and Drugs, we can identify four key metrics and focal points of opportunity to improve the quality of Corporate Information Services efforts. These metrics are: **DQ/OQ/PQ/IQ**. (Design Quality, Operational Quality, Procedural Quality, and Implementation Quality)

We also use a Quality Score Card to measure the ongoing quality lifecycle of the project or application. There is a column for each of the Development Quality metrics as well as columns for the QA function and the post-implementation cycle.

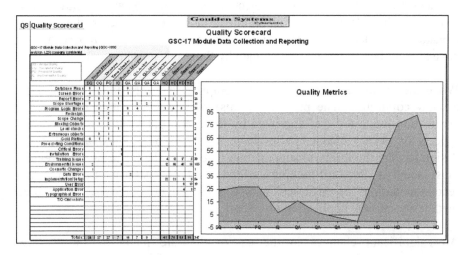

Please keep in mind that these first four design quality checkpoints MUST be performed before turning the application over to any formal QA function in order to have any level of significance.

DQ: Design Quality – As the name implies, this involves designing for quality before the programming even begins. This requires involvement of

139

the user in an iterative process whereby the development team partners with the user community to identify what the user and functional requirements are and what requests can be technologically achieved.

Normally, this function is performed by the project design team while working closely with sponsors, Business Analysts, and other Subject Matter Experts (SME). This is an iterative process wherein the design of the product and deliverables is refined and agreed upon by all parties.

This process begins after a user request has been received by the Information Services department. Commonly referred to as the fact-finding stage, it involves open discussion and cooperation to clearly identify what the user community requires and melding those requirements with the Information Services standards and Corporate goals that will produce an application or system that functions reliably within the current and future Information Services environment. Flexibility and adaptability are key criteria during this phase. In this phase, screen and report mock-ups are presented and iteratively modified until all requirements have been achieved, including Information Service design standards.

When a consensus has been achieved among the user and developer community, the drafts are signed by the user sponsor and the Information Services representative and the project scope document can be drafted. The process is then documented, including project scope, process flow, Work Breakdown Structures (WBS). The mock-ups of screen and report layouts have already been approved and signed by the users and sponsors.

When the documentation package is complete, it is presented to a Design Review committee. The purpose of this committee is not to redesign the application requested and approved by the users, but to ensure that critical aspects of design characteristics have not been overlooked and that the design has the flexibility to support future needs of the business. This review must adopt a 'forward-looking' attitude and not base its decisions and recommendations on historical perspectives. To do otherwise is to force mediocrity into the application or system.

Any significant changes in the design that are made by the Review Committee must be approved by the user sponsor. These changes should be limited to standardization, flexibility, and utility, and not based on how thing have been done in the past.

Once the Review Committee and the User Sponsor agree to the design, it can be turned over to the development team. At this point, the Design Quality (**DQ**) metric measurements begin. As the development team begins work, there may be design flaws or shortages that come to light as those with more detailed knowledge get involved. Any design changes discovered and suggested by the development team should be recorded on the score card by the Project Manager.

PQ: Procedural Quality – The core theme behind defining Programming Quality is the enforcement of clearly defined programming standards. Modularity and code re-usability are critical success factors.

This level of quality is incorporated by the developers and their managers.

While the definition of the standards is incumbent upon the Information Services Management team, the actual implementation rests in the hands of the developers. There must be management oversight and involvement to ensure that the standards are being followed.

With the implementation of standards and pre-defined common modules, the foundation of every program will be established and the developer can concentrate on the business logic rather than continually spending time developing repetitious routines. The corollary to this is that the basic flow and navigation of every program will work exactly the same, reducing the effort required to test in the QA areas.

As the development team continues work of the product or application, structural flaws mar become apparent. Additional modules or programs may be affected that were not identified in earlier stages. These discoveries and observations may require changes to the scope that must be approved by the sponsors, since these changes may impact the Cost and Time Baselines. Procedural Quality (**PQ**) focuses on the individual components that make up the entire application or product.

OQ: Operational Quality – Operational Quality ensures that the components of the application or system will interact as the users expect when it is delivered. Typically, this is an iterative process performed by the members of the development team. Any issues requiring correction are coordinated among themselves for resolution. However, the Project Manager must be informed of any issues, which must be recorded in the Operational Quality (**OQ**) section of the score card. Issues discovered at this stage in the Development Quality cycle could indicate serious design flaws, and should be documented for future efforts.

If any significant changes to the design or functionality of the system or application are identified and recommended by the OQ team, it should be reviewed and approved by the Sponsors, users, and the Review Committee to ensure that the changes will satisfy the needs of the user, adhere to standards, and maintain the flexibility to support future needs of the business. Close attention to the Cost and Time Baselines must be maintained.

IQ: Implementation Quality – The final component of the development quality definition is at the installation level. Normally, this is performed by a team that is responsible for documentation, training, packaging, and installation. By segregating this group from development and Quality Assurance, a fourth level of quality checking is applied to the overall development process. It is not uncommon for members of this team to discover problems and issues that were over-looked by the users, developers, and QA team.

By combining the different viewpoints from these distinctive team members, we can provide a closer view of what the actual end-user will see and experience. With some control and monitoring, this provides a final point to eliminated errors and flaws before going through a formal QA process.

The first step in the process is performed by the Project Manager, who must ensure that all documentation is correct and matches the application; that the application actually functions in accordance with the defined functional requirements; and that the supporting turnover documentation will allow other members of the IQ team to perform their assessment and functional responsibilities. Any flaws or omissions discovered by the Project Manager should be recorded on the score card in the Implementation Quality (**IQ**) column and returned to the development team to make the necessary corrections.

QA: Quality Assurance -

This requires establishing standard test scripts to test each application or system by approved criteria.

Typically, this is an iterative process performed by the members of the Quality Assurance team. Any issues requiring correction are coordinated with the developers for resolution. If any significant changes to the design or functionality of the system or application are identified and recommended by the QA team, it should be reviewed and approved by the Sponsors, users, and the Review Committee to ensure that the changes will satisfy the needs of the user, adhere to standards, and maintain the flexibility to support future needs of the business.

In any event, all defects identified by the QA team must be recorded on the score card by the Project Manager.

The defects identified by the QA team will illustrate areas of improvement for the design and development teams and areas where they need additional work on their testing procedures.

It is important to note that at the end of the fourth QA cycle, the results ONLY indicate the perception of the Project Quality from the standpoint of the development and QA teams. At this point, the user perception is not available.

Post-Implementation Evaluation -

We take the stance that the first month after implementation of a project or application; it is still under the auspices of Project Management and the full ownership of the Project Manager. This provides a better framework to determine our overall project performance.

It is very common for an application or project to be delivered to the user community, thinking that the resulting product is feature-rich, easy to use, and meets the needs of the user. However, until the time the product is in the hands of the end-users, the Project manager has absolutely no metric to determine the value of the product to the user community. That is why the Post-Implementation Evaluation is essential.

It is incumbent upon the Project Manager to track all project or application problems that are experienced by the users during this first four week period. This allows the Project manager to identify design flaws or shortfalls as well as providing a mechanism to track the effectiveness of the Quality Assurance and Training & Documentation teams. By keeping the project 'open' during the first four weeks of implementation, we can gather valuable information to improve future efforts. While this extends the Cost and Time baselines a bit, it should be accounted for in the initial budgeting and scheduling processes.

The Project Manager should track each problem on a weekly basis. The completed Project Score Card with graphic and supporting line items should be a fundamental document used in the Project Close-out meetings. It is not a 'punitive' tool, but a broad 'how did we really do' versus what we think we did.

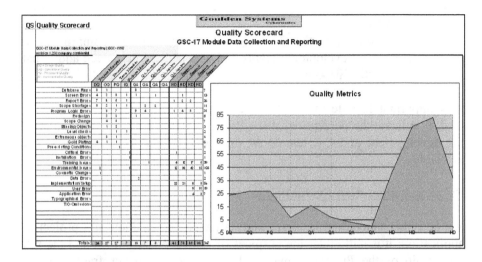

The final score card can be invaluable in identifying shortages in the quality lifecycle. In this instance, the developers discovered issues after the design approval, and had to go back to the review team and Sponsors to get those design shortages included in the scope.

After turning it over to QA, the four-week QA cycle found relatively few defects before handing it over to the Training, Documentation, and Implementation teams. Upon initial implementation, the number of flaws and problems escalated quickly. This could indicate to the Project Manager that better oversight is required on the QA, Training, and Documentation processes.

Finally, this graph clearly indicates the differing viewpoints of the Development and QA teams when contrasted with the views of the end-users. At the end of the QA cycle, the defect count was near zero. During the first week of implementation, the errors escalated to over forty, much higher than any point during the development/testing cycle.

With an unbiased and open dialogue at the Project Close-out meeting, each functional manage may see areas of improvement. Even if the Project Manager categorizes an error incorrectly, the counts will remain the same, illustrating the overall quality of the project from the viewpoint of the end-user.

In summary, Designing for Quality requires:
1. Use of four additional quality metrics beyond the typical Quality Assurance team;
   a. **Design Quality** –
   b. **Operational Quality** -

      c.   **Procedural Quality** -

      d.   **Implementation Quality** -

2. Accurately track, categorize, and record every flaw, shortfall, defect, error, and bug.

3. Use the Quality Score Card to monitor and report the Project Quality Progress.

4. Inclusion of the Post Implementation cycle as a Quality metric on all projects

The white paper, "Quality by Design", is available for viewing and downloads at:

http://www.projectperfect.com.au/info_quality_by_design.php

It has been included in this book by their kind permission.

INDEX

Coming Soon
From
Ronald Goulden

Non-Fiction	ISBN	Price
Project Management for a Functional World	1449996590	$39.95
Excel Tips with the Quality Scorecard	1450557155	$ 9.00
Excel: Scope, Charter, Executive Summary		
Excel: WBS, Cost Baseline, & Requirements		
Excel: Budget, Time, EVM, & PERT		
Excel: Time-keeping, Post Mortem, & Reviews		
Project Management: Tools, Tips, and Techniques		
The Interview		
The Book of Vex		
Survival		

www.ingramcontent.com/pod-product-compliance
Lightning Source LLC
Chambersburg PA
CBHW071203050326
40689CB00011B/2226